Matching Food and Wine

Also by Sandy O'Byrne

The Irish Table
Easons 1985

With Jacinta Delahaye
Wining and Dining at Home in Ireland
A. & A. Farmar 1994

Matching Food and Wine

Sandy O'Byrne

A. & A. Farmar

British Library Cataloguing in Publication Data
A CIP catalogue record for this book is available from the British Library

Decorations by Jacques Teljeur
Cover design by Bluett
Cover photographs by Walter Pfeiffer,
courtesy of Bord Bia/Irish Food Board
Typesetting and text layout by A. & A. Farmar
Printed and bound by Betaprint

ISBN 1 899047 32 8

A. & A. Farmar
Beech House
78 Ranelagh Village
Dublin 6
Ireland

Acknowledgments

I would like to thank the Wine Development Board, especially David Dillon and Jean Smullen, for giving me the opportunity to set up the Wine and Food course that was the origins of this book, and for their encouragement in its development.

I am grateful also to Anna and Tony Farmar for their professional expertise as publishers and for their personal support and encouragement during the writing of this book

Finally, thanks to my family and friends who, willingly or not, became invaluable 'guinea pigs' for matching food and wine!

Sandy O'Byrne
October 1997

CONTENTS

INTRODUCTION

There are two kinds of drinks. Some, such as whiskey and beer, are designed largely to be drunk by themselves, without any accompaniments. Others, such as wine (with the possible exception of Champagne), were created mainly to be drunk with food. The intimate association of wine and food—in which neither can be properly appreciated without the other—comes, if anything, as a surprise to northerners, whose traditions do not associate any one alcoholic drink so closely with food. The nearest analogy we have is tea, which seems to cry out for some kind of food, even if only a biscuit. The association obviously has implications for the way we should assess wine: when Monsieur Delmas, manager of the Bordeaux first-growth Château Haut-Brion was told that in a comparative tasting Château Lafite had performed better, he simply responded that Haut-Brion was designed to be drunk with meals, not with Château Lafite.

In history, winemaking belongs to Europe and certain parts of Asia. In European tradition wine was intended to be drunk at meals—it was not the highly taxed luxury or subject of deep study that it has sometimes become since. Wine was drunk for its taste, for its ability to enhance life and enrich the spirit, but above all to accompany food.

In the wine-producing regions of Europe themselves winemaking and cooking have evolved together over the centuries to produce the very best combinations of food and wine. No matter how unlikely, local partnerships have stood the test of time and invariably work. Think of Pauillac and roast lamb or the unexpected taste of sardines and the teeth-tingling acidity of *red*

Vinho Verde in Portugal. Such partnerships vary from region to region. For example, in Tuscany robust, mature red Chianti Riserva is served with game, whereas in Alsace a full, off-dry, rich white wine from Gewürztraminer or Pinot Gris is the most likely choice. That both combinations work, and can be appreciated and enjoyed by an outsider, points to some underlying harmony and rationale. It also shows that food and wine can be compatible in different ways: that there is always more than one wine to suit any dish.

One reason why regional food and wines make such successful matches is that the range of either is limited, and over centuries a consistency has evolved between food and wine traditions. Wine and food are both agricultural products, and those from the same area share the same climate, soil and environment as well as similar traditions of cultivation. For example, wines from hot regions, especially those of the Mediterranean, have riper, richer flavours than those of the cooler north in the same way that vegetables and fruit are more flavoursome and local herbs and strong tasting olive oil are more liberally used.

In France's regional gastronomy it is the method of cooking as much as the ingredients which influence the choice of wine. The fine wine regions have refined but relatively simple traditional cuisines, while the most vibrant and complex cuisines appear alongside simpler wines. In Bordeaux, for instance, cooking is based on meats such as local lamb, duck and guinea fowl with delicate classic sauces to show off the finest bottles of the Haut Médoc. Burgundy's cuisine is richer but still refined, concentrated on long-simmered meat dishes and rich, dark wine sauces which benefit from the extra spice and acidity of the Pinot Noir.

In the restaurants of Lyon, some of the country's finest and most innovative, Beaujolais is the most likely accompaniment to the rich and daring food. In the south of France, where herbs, garlic and robust daubes and cassoulets abound, wines are fruitier

han the classic structured wines of Bordeaux and have spicy and
arthy flavours.

The rich cookery of Alsace is set against a panorama of dry,
trong and aromatic white wines, which provide a perfect coun-
erbalance for the dairy products, cured meats and foie gras of the
egion. Think of the rich onion tart emerging wobbling and
neltingly creamy from the oven set against the brilliant crisp fruit
f a Riesling; of pungent, tangy Munster cheese with spicy
Gewürztraminer and of unctuous foie gras with a late-harvested,
picy, off-dry Pinot Gris.

In the Loire, another essentially white wine area, you find the
pungent crottin de chèvre with alternatively minerally or smoky
Sauvignons of Sancerre and Pouilly-Fumé. Further west, the
reamy, tangy goats' cheese of Sainte-Maure matches the local
Vouvrays. Dry, crisp, full white wines from the Chenin Blanc
work well with fish like *sandre*, while by the coast Muscadet is the
perfect, fresh, yeasty choice for Nantais mussels.

The rich cuisine of the Périgord with its truffles and foie gras,
its walnuts and goose fat, finds the right foil in the simpler wines
of Bordeaux and especially in the reds of Bergerac and Cahors.
Further south, cassoulets of beans, sausage, preserved duck and
pork, are best with the fruitier styles of neighbouring Corbières.

In Provence there are 'winter and summer wines'. In summer
resh, vibrant, dry rosés are perfect with grilled fish, vegetable
alads and all the little dishes of the region while the strong
powerful reds of Bandol and the Southern Rhône complement
he rich hearty casseroles and daubes of meat and game which
warm the months of the mistral.

In Italy food and wine have a special affinity, though less clearly
defined than in France. Here, from the mountains of Piedmont
o the Veneto, and from the Renaissance splendour of Tuscany to
he isolated villages of Puglia, wine is as much a part of daily
meals as a loaf of bread. This is wine to drink without fuss—

sturdy and robust, dry and savoury, made from its own grape varieties in its own style and too often misunderstood. Most red Italian wines are dry and fragrant, they do not shout the immediate fruit aromas and flavours beloved by today's wine world. They have tannin, and are often bitter or slightly astringent with tarry, smoky flavours of fruit and wood. Above all, they are appetising wines which demand food and greatly enhance the vigorous flavours of Italian regional fare.

In Tuscany the sharp, strong young Chiantis season plates of meat-based antipasti or pasta with mushrooms, while their more venerable cousins Chianti Riserva, Brunello and Vino Nobile di Montepulciano, accompany dishes of pigeon, beef or game. The reserve and austerity of the wine is the perfect foil to the rich flavours of the food. The everyday rossos, Barberas, Dolcettos and Montepulcianos, provide robust, dry and thoroughly appetising accompaniments to dishes such as pasta, polenta, veal or cheese. In fact, there is probably no better, simpler meal than such a wine served with good salami, olives and rough country bread. Further south in Italy, where meat and game give way to more pasta, vegetables and grain, the wines have a richer character with the ripe, dark flavours of sunny southern fruit and the taste of the scorching heat of summer. These are the perfect wines for olive oil, baked stuffed aubergines or spicy tomato sauces.

The white wines of Italy also have a particular role. They are often criticised as neutral, lacking fruit and aroma and general excitement. But they are intended only as crisp clean contrasts to seafood and vibrant, mixed antipasti, setting up the palate for something richer to follow. A colourful array of fennel, anchovies, smoked hams, olives, tomato salad, fresh or dried beans all scented with herbs, garlic and olive oil, does not need a fruit salad in the glass to accompany the myriad of tastes but rather a refreshing contrast such as Verdicchio, Frascati or Pinot Grigio can provide.

In northern Portugal, the dry, dusty, sometimes unapproachable wines match the dried cod, the chunky caldos and rich bean stews of that region in a way which is simple and perfect. Further south, colonial spices are more obvious in the food and the wines are more fruity—again the match is right. These are food and wine combinations which belong almost exclusively in the country of origin. Portuguese ingredients cannot be easily found or replicated abroad and increasingly wines for export have the edges rounded out and some of the magic is lost.

Certain wines have lost their food context altogether in exportation. In Jerez, they say God made seafood for fino sherry; but the export model, a sometimes sweetened and blander version, is more usually sipped alone. Yet, in Spain with the sun beating down, a plate of local shrimps and a bottle of cold fino is one of the greatest experiences of food and wine in the world.

These examples show how effectively the local culinary and winemaking traditions have evolved memorable partnerships: if we were simply to stick to cooking from one region, there would be no problem in associating appropriate wines. But that is not realistic. A generation ago paella, chow mein and prawns in tomato sauce were sufficiently exotic. Fresh ingredients were seasonal and localised and there was a limited number of spices and other seasonings in everyday use. Cooking styles were simpler, based on fish or meat, a few sauces and vegetables in a minor accompanying role. Professional cookery in hotels and restaurants was more or less confined to so-called classic—or international—interpretations of French cuisine. Now, food has also developed a cosmopolitan nature and, both at home and in restaurants, Chinese, Indian and Mediterranean dishes are more common than the traditional 'meat and two veg.'.

Apart from the range of individual types of cuisine, modern cooking is eclectic, mixing influences from different origins. In restaurants especially, single dishes may combine elements from French, Japanese, Thai and Mediterranean traditions. Oriental cooking does not come from a wine-drinking culture. Many of today's culinary toys like Thai spices, balsamic vinegar, salsas and designer risotto are challenging for wine, especially the more classic types. Duck à l'orange may have always been tricky to match perfectly with fine wine, but duck flavoured with five-spice and anise, served with couscous and roasted vegetables and a mango salsa, is a whole new world of tastes and flavours.

As the range of foods available has widened, so has the range of wines. The annual guide *The Best of Wine in Ireland* lists the 1,300 or so top quality and value wines available in Ireland—three bottles every day for a year to taste the lot—representing no more than the top half of the market. These wines come from France (of course) but also Germany, Austria, Italy, Spain, Portugal, Greece, Hungary, Bulgaria, South Africa, North and South America, Australia, New Zealand and even the Lebanon. Twenty or thirty years ago, the choice was nothing like so great. At the same time, the wine world is not only larger, it is also much less clearly divided in terms of regional style. Wines have been developed which are not immediately associated with a particular kind of local food. Similar grape varieties are grown in many different countries and a scientific understanding of winemaking has led to the same techniques being employed worldwide. The problem now is one of choice.

It is presumably no coincidence that as the eclectic cooking styles developed, so too did a new style of winemaking, with stronger, riper fruit flavours than the more structured and austere classic wines of Europe. Wine regions like California, Australia and New Zealand have developed their modern wine industries in a new environment unrestricted by tradition or legislation. Their emphasis is on ripe, aromatic fruit which is the best possible example of the grape variety. Specifically modern wine-making, now not necessarily confined to New World countries, produces wines with more obvious fruit aromas, softer tannins in red wines, riper fruit, more concentration and consequently higher lcohol. Australian Shiraz can be excellent with hot, spicy food; New Zealand Sauvignon Blanc with ripe Mediterranean vegetables; Zinfandel with zingy barbecue tastes and ripe overblown Hunter Valley Chardonnay with the spice and coconut of a Thai curry. Some of these super-rich wines do not combine well with the richness and subtlety of classical cooking which needs the savoury bite of tannin, the acidity and austerity of classic wines made in a style which assumes that food is the missing part of the equation.

The old ideas about matching wine and food were devised for a smaller planet and related to clearly defined and limited assumptions about both the wine and the food. The basic rule of white wine for fish and white meat, and red wine for red meat and game was based on the equation of tannin/acidity of wine with the protein/fat of food. This is still often accurate, but is really no more than a convenient (and easily memorised) colour code for the way things usually work out.

By nature, most white wines are lighter than reds, with less oak, extract and a lack of tannin. Their weight balances the texture of foods such as fish, chicken and veal which are themselves delicate and easily overpowered by a full-bodied wine. The weight of the wine and food should be in balance, and this, rather than the colour is the most important factor.

Light red wines, such as Beaujolais, are fine with delicate food. A meaty dish like mullet can suit a light to medium bodied red wine such as Pinot Noir.

Firm tannin in a wine is damaging to fish which lacks the fatty, protective tissue of meat and brings out the astringency of the wine resulting in a metallic taste.

The purpose of this book is to explain and illustrate with recipes the principles that govern successful combination of food and wine. Done well, as we have seen, the combination brings out the best in both. Done carelessly, the palate is left struggling with clashing flavours and sensations. A clash between wine and food occurs when the sense of taste is reduced or distorted by one or the other. A complex wine, one which is fine and mature, with layers of taste, is hard to absorb with a dish which has many strong flavours. Consequently, the finest wines are often served with the simplest food and this presents a persistent dilemma for creative cooks who are also wine buffs. For example, roast lamb is a traditional, classic accompaniment to top Médoc wines. But if you add a herb crust, perhaps a tapenade, or another garlicky sauce, a garnish of vegetables with olive oil, then you should stick to a simpler wine, a young straightforward Médoc or something from further south which is vigorous and direct in taste. Your palate cannot cope with complexity both in the glass and on the plate, and generally the more obvious food tastes will win out over those in an expensive bottle of wine.

2 WHY WINE TASTES AS IT DOES

To enjoy food and wine fully, you need to be able to taste both; that is, the tastes of each should complement the other in a way that the palate and other senses can appreciate. That is why the balance of weights is of first importance.

To understand the process one needs to know a little about how the sense of taste works. Strictly speaking, 'taste' is confined to the palate or tastebuds, which can identify four main types: sweet, salt, acid and bitter. The palate also feels things like weight, texture, temperature and astringency. The texture of food varies from ingredient to ingredient, and also from one cooking method to another. Other factors influencing the enjoyment of food and wine include sight, touch and, most of all, smell.

The sense of smell, although separate, is in fact the most important and sensitive part of the ability to taste. Over time it develops into a system of reference and recognition. When you taste a wine or food, your sense of smell acts with that of taste to expand the flavour in your mouth. Taste and aroma are so closely linked that flavour is really a combination of the two. Pungent smells in the environment can dramatically influence the way something tastes: eating at a freshly polished table can have disastrous effects on the flavour of food! More commonly, the lack of a sense of smell due to a head cold makes tasting very difficult and limited. Because the sense of smell is built over time, familiarity is important: the more you taste the more aware you become of comparisons and contrasts and the wider range of flavours you recognise in both food and wine. Aromas are the easiest sensations to remember, recall and associate with past experience. An aroma does not last as long as a taste—as soon as you become accustomed to a particular aroma it loses intensity; this is where taste, and most importantly length of flavour, takes over.

Wine can be categorised by a variety of criteria: colour, whether it is light or liqueur, still or sparkling, and also by origin, price and so on. Any classification is arbitrary and certain wines can cross boundaries depending on the vintage or the maker. Above all, wine is a natural product. Viticulture is farming and the vine a Mediterranean plant cultivated over centuries to provide sustenance and pleasure for humanity. Its ultimate style and taste come from a particular environment and the way in which it is manipulated. A wine varies from one vineyard to another, from year to year and even between individual bottles, this is its charm and its frustration. Such variety also means that a wine can be found for almost any food, while at the same time, the range of choice presents a challenge.

In each region, and between different makers, the importance of individual factors varies. In many regions winemaking practices are laid down by law to preserve the traditional character and established quality of wine from a certain area. In new regions there is more freedom for the winemaker to act depending on his or her intention for the wine in terms of style and price: he or she can choose to make a simple varietal expressing the primary character of one grape variety, or to produce a blend from different regions or grape varieties.

The grape is influenced by its natural environment or terroir—the climate, soil, local conditions and annual weather—and by the way it is handled, by the cultivation of the vine and the winemaking itself. All wine vines need a climate with definite seasons, which gives a period of winter rest essential for the following year's growth. Within this general climatic band climates vary from the cool, marginal conditions of northern Germany to the hot, sun-scorched vineyards of the Hunter Valley. The biggest distinction is between cool and hot climate fruit. Long, slow ripening at very moderate temperatures leads to high acidity and less ripe fruit flavours in white wines, typified by Rhine or Mosel Riesling and the wines of Sancerre and Pouilly-Fumé. Warm, temperate climates build firm tannins and the concentrated fruit of long-term reds such as those of Bordeaux, where the seaboard modifies a more southern climate. Hot countries produce very ripe fruit with plentiful alcohol and rich flavours. Tannin and acidity are lower and earthy, and spicy aromas abound as in Châteauneuf-du-Pape. In much of northern Europe the climate is marginal for ripening grapes and the weather in individual years will have a marked effect on the wine produced, whereas in a country like Chile weather patterns are more consistent and the winemaking or vinification methods of the individual may be the most marked influence. In a small region like Chablis the actual soil of the vineyards may be the most significant factor in creating a unique style of wine.

However, modern winemaking has considerable ability to control the natural process of viticulture and vinification, to modify or emphasise effects of climates or vintage. The amount of alcohol and fruit impact can be controlled or exaggerated by the ripeness of the grapes and the degree of intervention in the vinification. Certain wines may be fermented or aged in oak, or otherwise matured to add additional flavours of wood and age which will eventually knit together in a complex whole.

The quality of a wine may be defined by its balance in *flavour* and *structure*. Flavour is provided by the grape, the type of winemaking and the time spent in the bottle. Structure in turn is made up of six elements: sweetness, acidity, tannin, oak, body and alcohol.

Flavour

Flavour is the most specific characteristic of a food or wine. Flavours are individual, varied and can be combined in different ways to achieve contrast, harmony, etc. *Flavour type* is the individual flavour of a particular wine. Flavours in wine can be primary (grape), secondary (winemaking and oak) or tertiary (age). There needs to be both balance and contrast between the actual flavour of the wine and that of the food. This can be achieved through direct contrast such as the sweet/salt of Sauternes and Roquefort, or through the more harmonious balance of lamb and Médoc, refreshing Chablis and oysters or enriching Burgundy and game. Strong foods and seasoning need similarly vigorous wines, for example, goats' cheese is better with a Sauvignon-based wine than a Muscadet.

Intensity of flavour comes from the concentration and ripeness of the grapes, the particular grape variety and the winemaking process. A wine can be immediately intense or upfront in flavour or it may be more subtle and complex, in which case the flavour emerges more slowly and develops as you taste the wine. The intensity of a flavour, as well as the actual type of flavour, needs to be balanced between food and wine in the same way as weight so that one does not overpower the other. For example, Châteauneuf-du-Pape is too strong in taste for chicken with tarragon. Compare too a Chilean Merlot and a Pomerol: the first has a very intense attack of ripe fruit, which is strong and vibrant and matches strongly flavoured food like barbecued chicken. The Pomerol is also intense but the flavour emerges more slowly and is better suited to strong but more integrated flavours like game. Food which is more complex in terms of ingredients, not style of cooking, needs wine which has an obvious and immediate flavour. For example, the many flavours of a pizza are complemented by the vigorous fruit of a Dolcetto. Simpler food, and foods with more integrated flavours, match wines with layers of taste such as a fine Burgundy with roast pheasant.

A key factor in assessing the intensity of the wine is the finish or after-taste and the time the flavour persists or lasts after you drink it. Certain wines have a very long finish which can work well with intensely flavoured food, as the two tastes follow one another. A good example is Champagne with Oriental food—the acidity and sparkle of the wine is refreshing, while the flavours follow afterwards when the immediate impact of the food has faded.

The first principles in matching food and wine should be to balance the weight and intensity of each with the other, and to offset richness or complexity in one with austerity or directness of flavour in the other.

The *grape variety* is the primary factor determining the taste of a wine. The influence of the grape is especially important today with increased emphasis on varietal character, the number of single variety wines produced and the international spread of popular grapes. Although different conditions and handling will alter the style of the same grape, certain characteristics will always stand out, especially those of the noble grape varieties. For example, Cabernet Sauvignon is now grown throughout the world and displays different amounts of fruit, longevity and complexity in different environments. However, Cabernet is never as soft and immediate as Merlot can be; it always shows rather reserved blackcurrant fruit, a classic whiff of cedar and a slightly unyielding structure which is a dry, austere, often intriguingly complex accompaniment to food. Apart from individual flavours, different grape varieties have different amounts of potential alcohol, acidity, tannin etc which give structure and general style to a particular wine. The noble or classic grape varieties demonstrate their individual character most strongly of all. In spite of variations, the grape variety can be a useful starting point to match wine with food.

Two other general factors affect the flavour of the wine and therefore its suitability for matching with this food or that. These are the style of *winemaking* (including the winemaker's reaction to environmental factors such as climate and terroir) and age. Within obvious limits—you cannot get super-ripe high alcohol full-bodied reds from the Mosel, or vibrant, high-acidity whites from the Southern Rhône—the style of winemaking can crucially affect the outcome. For instance, of two winemakers growing Sauvignon Blanc, one may decide to aim for a fruity varietal taste, and tightly control the maceration, use a selected yeast, very cool fermentation etc., whereas another may use natural yeast, or blend the output of several terroirs to produce a more typical, less varietal, style.

The other factor that affects flavour is *age*. Over time the fruit slowly declines, the structure softens and other flavours develop. A young wine presents an aggressively fruity nose, whereas the older wine tends to be mellower, softer and more harmonious.

Structure

The structure of the wine may be described as the canvas on which the flavours are the colours. The six elements that make up structure—sweetness, acidity, tannin, oak, body and alcohol—are combined by the winemaker in various combinations of intensity to allow the flavours to show to best advantage.

Sweetness in wine comes from residual sugar of ripe or very ripe grapes, e.g. Vouvray Moelleux and Beerenauslese, or from added grape must or sussreserve. High alcohol can give an impression of sweetness, e.g. Zinfandel. Intensity of fruit can be confused with sweetness in a wine which has little or no residual sugar, e.g. New Zealand Sauvignon Blanc.

Sweetness in wine can complement sweet food, but also certain savoury dishes. For sweet foods the wine must be as sweet or sweeter than the food it accompanies because:

i) wine has balancing acidity; ii) sweetness of wine is from ripe grapes not pure sugar.

Sweeter wines can work with savoury foods which are either very rich e.g. foie gras, or salty e.g. blue cheese. Certain savoury foods, especially fish and vegetables, have hidden sweetness which is complemented by off-dry or medium sweet wines with crisp acidity, e.g. scallops and Spätlese. Spicy dishes are good with sweetness, e.g. wontons and Auslese.

Acidity is essential to all wine: it acts as a preservative, enhances the aroma, adds bite and finish and stimulates appetite. Dry white wine therefore is the perfect apéritif. The richness of an ingredient, or a method of cooking such as frying, or added fat like butter, olive oil or a sauce, call for acidity. It is the same as squeezing lemon on to deep-fried fish—or vinegar on chips. The sharpness of the lemon or wine stimulates the palate; it literally makes your mouth water, and so cuts the cloying effects of fat so that the other flavours of the food can be tasted. Good examples of this effective type of combination include Muscadet and mussels, Frascati and fried fish.

Acidity is high or crisp in cool climate white wines, typically those from Riesling, Sauvignon Blanc or Chenin Blanc grape varieties, and also in Italian and Portuguese reds. Tannin can mask acidity so acidity may be very high in notably tannic wines like Barolo. Acidity also offsets residual sugar in wines such as Coteaux du Layon, making them refreshing and palatable in spite of great sweetness. Wines with low acidity such as some Gewürztraminer and Viognier are relatively difficult to combine with food.

Tannin is found in red wines, principally those intended to age. It comes from the skins and stalks of grapes and the wood tannins in barrels. It is bitter and astringent in taste and dries the palate—to sandpaper in the case of a really tannic wine. Moderate amounts give structure and bite and some austerity to wine.

Classic varietals and food

Whites	Characteristics	Suitable foods
Riesling	Dry to sweet, high acidity, light to medium body, fine and aromatic, ages well.	Dry: delicate foods like fish, richness in sauces, cooking methods and ingredients. Off-dry: spices. Light aromatic: rich sauces.
Chardonnay	Balanced acidity, medium to full body, usually oaked. Varying amount of oak. Apple, peach, melon-type fruit, creamy and buttery, with toasted influence, medium to high alcohol.	Main courses, fish with sauces, chicken and light meats, smoked foods, fruit-influenced savoury dishes, pasta with cream sauces, creamy cheeses.
Sémillon	Dry or sweet and botrytized, full-bodied, waxy, honeyed character with citrus-type fruit acidity when young.	Dry: textured fish, chicken and light meats, spices, Chinese dishes. Sweet: nutty puddings, light cakes and pastries, blue cheese, foie gras and similar rich pâtés.
Sauvignon Blanc	Dry, crisp acidity, medium body, very aromatic and intense, from gooseberry to green apple, citrus type fruit to limes, green peppers and grassy influences. Classically minerally, flinty overtones.	Well-flavoured fish, some chicken and light meats, vegetable and tomato based pasta, smoked salmon, spicy and herb flavoured food, goats' cheese, some blue cheese and strong cheeses in general.
Chenin Blanc	Dry to sweet, high acidity, medium to full-bodied, aromatic citrus, apple, floral and honeyed fruit, ages well.	Dry: rich food e.g. fish with sauces, pâté and charcuterie, salads and some spices. Sweet: some spicy savoury food, goats' cheese and strong cheeses; also fruit-based puddings.

Reds	Characteristics	Suitable foods
Cabernet Sauvignon	Tannin, medium acidity, full body, typically blackcurrant-type fruit with mint, cedar and cigar-like aromas, ages well.	Protein, especially red meat, matches rich meats like lamb and duck, rich meat sauces and game like widgeon.
Pinot Noir	Medium tannin, medium to upper acidity, elegant body, rich fruit, typically strawberry type with spicy overtones, develops gamey vegetal character, moderate to long ageing.	Red meat and some cheeses, typically game or beef, also casseroles and wine-based sauces. Lighter, fruity styles with textured fish, some spices and mushroom pasta or risotto.
Syrah	Tannin, acidity, high alcohol, full body, can be firm and dense in structure or rich and fruit-driven, dark fruit character of brambles, dark plums, violets with very spicy peppery overtones, ages well.	Depends on structure and tannin, red meat, grilled and barbecued meats, game, casseroles, substantial pasta and grain-based dishes which include meat; richer styles can match spicy food.
Merlot	Low to moderate tannin, higher alcohol, medium to full body, ripe, rich fruit character typically raspberries, plums and chocolate, can be fruity and simple or layered, rich and complex, ageing depends on style, generally moderate.	Depends on tannin and oak influence, meats like beef, game like quail, pasta dishes and vegetarian food if not too oaky. Sausages, salamis and pâtés with fruity versions, some cheeses.

The drying qualities of tannin stimulate appetite and particularly complement the protein of red meats. Meat textures get the palate working while the fat protects it from the harsher effects of tannin: the wine immediately appears softer and other flavours more obvious. Rich, densely textured foods like game also benefit from the tannin, which balances their intense, gamey flavour. As it adds structure, tannin needs food with weight and texture as well as richness or fat, e.g. meats like beef or lamb, whereas with a delicate, low fat food like fish, it can create a harsh, almost metallic taste. Lighter red wines, and those with softer tannins can be drunk with fish, especially dishes like chunky roasted cod, salmon or grilled mullet. Light, modern, fat-reduced cooking, often based on vegetables and grains rather than meat, needs much softer wines, more fruit and lower tannin. Spicy flavours increase the impact of the tannin as both are bitter. Hot spices, like chilli which contains tannin of its own, make wine seem more harsh and tannic than ever. Salt also tends to increase the impact of tannin, though smoked food, which is actually sweeter, can have the opposite effect.

Oak barrels are used to mature wine. Wood ageing gives the wine structure and flavour and starts the ageing process during which the tannins soften and the fruit integrates with the flavours of the wood, developing more complex aromas and flavours of its own. A barrel has a life span of four years and the top wines will receive most or all new oak which has the strongest impact. Fine red wines therefore are aged in new *barriques*, the newest oak barrels. Lesser wines are aged in a mixture of new and one or two year-old barrels where the impact is not so strong. Oak adds structure and certain specific flavours to both red and white wine. To be aged in oak a wine needs plenty of fruit concentration and flavour of its own to stand up to the added effects of wood.

Different types of oak have different effects and add specific flavours. White wines fermented and aged in new *barriques* take on characteristic spicy, toasted, buttery qualities. Part of the effect is that oak-aged wines normally undergo malolactic fermentation, a chemical reaction occuring after the alcoholic fermentation by which harsh malic acid is converted to softer lactic acid so lowering the overall acidity of the wine. It also contributes to the buttery, creamy quality, as in Meursault. Similar effects are obtained by barrel-ageing only, as opposed to fermentation, although sometimes the oak is more obvious in the finished wine.

Oak adds body to wine which therefore needs to be equalled by the texture, weight and richness of the food it accompanies. Oak tannins add dryness which reacts well to richness and to sauces in particular. Oak flavours—toast, caramel, vanilla, spice, smoke etc —are strong and need strong food flavours, especially if the oak is pronounced or the wine is young. The strength of flavour needed in the food depends on the integration of the oak. Obvious oak is a dominant taste and needs very flavoursome food, generally strong and vigourous in taste rather than complex. More integrated oak takes well to rich, classic flavours. Because of the drying effect and the oaky bite, such wines are less good with vegetables and simply cooked fish than with richer foods. The tannin in oak also tends to clash with hot spices.

The *body* is the way the wine feels in the mouth, a combination of sugar, extract, alcohol and intensity. The body of the wine should be approximately equal the texture and substance of the food. Wines from hotter climates tend to have more body than those from the north.

Alcohol in table wine is legally between 8.5 and 16.5 per cent by volume. The level adds to the body and weight of the wine, giving a fuller mouth feel. Compare a Mosel Kabinett Riesling and an Alsace Riesling, for example. Alcohol also gives a sense of sweetness and balances acidity in wine. High alcohol can give a burning sensation at the back of the mouth. High alcohol wines generally complement foods with both texture and strength of flavour. The rich/sweet effect is especially good with strongly flavoured and smoked foods and certain cheeses.

The key to a good combination of food and wine is balance. A clear understanding of the characteristics of the wine and the food (especially the cooking methods) is necessary to achieve that balance. The various elements in wine, such as body, sweetness and flavour should be matched with those in the food. Thus the weight or body of the wine should be related to the texture of the main ingredient of the dish—so that one does not serve a delicate light red with steak and onions, or a full-bodied heavily oaked chardonnay with a light delicate fish dish. Other factors such as acidity and sweetness must also be considered.

Finally, it is important to be clear that the wine goes with the dish, not with the food. Thus to say that Cabernet Sauvignon goes well with lamb is broadly true. However, it does ignore important factors such as the winemaking style, or the age and cooking style of the lamb. The old French view of wine as the second sauce is helpful in matching flavours. If you consider the kind of sauce flavours that might be appropriate, those are the wine flavours too. The analogy is as simple as a crisp dry white wine with fried fish rather than lemon juice, or a spicy Northern Rhône instead of mustard with saute of beef.

Cooking methods

Although certain ingredients such as cheese, olives and oysters can be eaten on their own, most food involves a combination of ingredients, a method of cooking and various seasonings, sauces and garnishes which combine to produce an end flavour, so that wine is more readily matched to a dish than to one of its constituents. For example, a simply roasted chicken is perfect with white Burgundy, but when cut up and browned, then cooked in a rich mushroom sauce, a red wine like St Émilion would be better. Stir-fried chicken with ginger or a casserole with peppers and rice would call for yet other wines.

The changes a food undergoes during cooking affect the style of wine that will best complement the finished dish. Cooking methods are therefore an important consideration when choosing wine. Whether or not an ingredient has been browned is the first point to consider.

The brown colour comes from caramelised sugars and immediately changes and strengthens the flavour. Because *browning* requires high, direct heat, muscle tissue seizes and increases in texture: charcoal grilling is the most obvious example, though roasting, pan-frying and baking also add texture and flavour. When selecting wine, whether or not a meat has been browned makes a great difference. Take, for example, the difference between poached and grilled chicken: the former needs the most delicate of white wines, the second would happily partner a Chardonnay or even a fruity red. Barbecued or charcoal-grilled food is excellent with oaky, fruit-driven, warm country wines.

Poaching and steaming are the most delicate methods of cooking and on the whole produce very delicate food. The style of dish comes from the accompaniments or flavourings, for example, the aromatics in a bouillon for salmon, the spices in Oriental steamed fish or in Middle Eastern couscous. Even the most robust of steamed dishes, such as couscous, is better with light to medium-bodied wines, with moderate tannin and plenty of fruit.

Braising, stewing and casseroling are the most obvious methods of cooking by exchange, a process whereby flavours are extracted from the main ingredient and others added. These methods often combine the browning process with long slow simmering with other flavours like vegetables, herbs and wine. They are good wine dishes as they have plenty of texture and the flavours are integrated and harmonious, even if relatively strong. Meat casseroles go well with medium to full-bodied reds and take well to oaky flavours, high acidity and youthful vigour.

Pan-fried dishes and stir-fries, although mixed dishes, tend to have a lighter, finer consistency and less integrated flavour than anything braised. In pan-fried dishes the sauce, as well as the strength of other ingredients, plays a major role in shaping the flavour. In mixed dishes such as these wine becomes one of a number of flavours and needs good character of its own to win out. In general oak, varietal character and some individual varieties and ripe fruit all work well with pan-fried and stir-fried foods. Deep-fried foods are generally crisp and light in texture, though quite rich. Clean, crisp acidity and light to medium body are essential. Generally white wines work best with deep-fried fish, though Italian reds in particular work with cheese or mushroom fritters.

Principal ingredients and accompaniments

Apart from the method of cooking, the ingredients used, the complexity of flavours and how well integrated they are all have a big effect on the choice of wine. Some dishes involve one principal ingredient with a sauce and garnish, which may be classically harmonious or may present various strong flavours. For example, pan-fried lamb with a sauce of wine, herbs and lamb juices is more harmonious in taste than marinated, grilled lamb with a relish. Other dishes such as casseroles, risotto and pasta dishes are composite. Or a number of individual dishes may be served together, as with Oriental food.

There are three factors to consider when matching *meat* and wine: texture, richness and flavour. The texture of meat requires a well-structured wine. All red meat is complemented by tannin, except when it is heavily spiced. Beef and venison have the most texture and the highest protein of all meats. Lamb has more fat than beef and is richer in taste, therefore it needs a contrast from the wine—something dry, savoury and reserved rather than rich and fleshy—Médoc rather than St Émilion, Cabernet rather than Merlot. Individual cuts have different strengths of flavour which need to be matched by the wine. For example, fillet of beef cut into elegant medallions is less robust than an entire rib, charcoal-grilled on the bone. A Californian Cabernet would complement the rib but the fillet could match a more mature, complex wine, such as an eight-year-old claret.

The texture of *poultry and game* varies from the delicate flesh of domestic fowl to the firmer flesh of wild fowl like pheasant. Waterfowl tend to be firm-fleshed, and turkey has a mixture of light, delicate white meat and more textured dark flesh. Wild fowl are usually lean, chicken and turkey have moderate fat, and duck and geese are very fatty indeed and need considerable acidity/tannin to balance this. Strength of flavour varies from mild chicken up to strong-tasting wild duck, which requires a wine of similar intensity. Flavour is also determined by cooking method and how long the game has been allowed to hang. Free-range chicken is one of the best possible foils to really fine wine with moderate tannin, such as red or white Burgundy. Rabbit is mild and goes well with light red wines with lively acidity, while hare is much richer and darker, and calls for a robust, spicy red wine.

Fish varies in texture from very delicate plaice to flakey fish like cod to meaty textured monkfish. White fish from northern waters is generally delicate in taste and texture.

Unless the dish has a very rich sauce, or is cooked in pastry, oak is not helpful, so choose an Alsace white, Sauvignon Blanc, Chablis or very lightly oaked Chardonnay. On the other hand richly cooked, textured fish is excellent with classic oaked wines. For example, turbot with a rich cream or hollandaise sauce is magnificent with Meursault and a well made fish-pie goes beautifully with Californian or cool climate Australian Chardonnay from Victoria or Western Australia.

Really meaty fish like monkfish, tuna or swordfish need more body in the wine, and often work well with a light or medium red. Tuna especially is good with New World Merlot or Italian Barbera.

Oily fish like sardines and herring present a real problem. Most of all they need high acidity which is the reason that Portuguese wines are often successful. Otherwise an Italian white or New Zealand Riesling, though nothing too fine, is the best solution.

Most *shellfish* is dense in texture and concentrated in protein. It is also rich in taste and needs acidity; an example is the classic combination of oysters and Chablis. Molluscs are tangy and rich in flavour and need the minerally, fresh acidity of Muscadet, Chablis, Vinho Verde or an understated Sauvignon like Entre-deux-Mers. Fresh, youthful Italian white wines also work very well.

Crustaceans such as crab and lobster are rich and sweet, and in he case of lobster have lots of texture. Crab is excellent with classic Riesling, or a young Chablis; lobster takes well to oaked Chardonnay, Burgundian or New World depending on its cooking.

Scallops are delicate and sweet but allow some exciting wine companions, even sweet Loire wines can be a magical accompaniment. Avoid oak because of the delicacy, but Riesling, young Chablis or Pinot Blanc are all successful.

River fish are rich though delicate in flavour. Salmon responds well to classic Chardonnay, the richer styles of Pouilly-Fumé or a southern Rhône or Australian Marsanne, as the fish is textured yet delicate. A light red wine, served slightly cool, is also good with salmon—especially if the fish has been baked or roasted. Chinon or Bourgueil from the Loire, or New World Pinot Noir are good choices.

Owing to their saltiness, *cured and dried meats* respond well to fruit and sweetness—think of ham with apple or redcurrant sauce. Baked or boiled ham is fairly easy with wine apart from very mature or austere reds which have too much complexity, tannin or body for the salty tastes of the meat. Any of the soft, fruity, spicy reds with which today's wine world is well supplied complement a fine glazed ham.

Air-dried ham such as comes from Parma or Bayonne is rather different: salted, dried or smoked ham is very intense in taste and needs a fresh, lively wine to accompany it—any lightly aromatic white wine from Verdicchio to Riesling Spätlese works well.

Salamis and various kinds of dried sausages have both flavour, often lots of garlic or spice, and high fat—so need acidity and fruit. Beaujolais and light reds go well with picnic sausages, so does dry, fruity rosé or varietal Merlot.

Raw sausages are also rich in fat and need plenty of acidity—Silvaner or Portuguese reds are excellent with various types of sausage casserole.

Black pudding is a popular starter but needs rather carefully chosen wine. Served with apples it goes well with a Spätlese or Vouvray, the earthier flavours of potatoes or lentils are probably better with a soft red like Rioja.

Grains, pasta and rice have an entirely different texture to protein foods, and have no fat in themselves, though they are frequently served with oily or fatty accompaniments. The texture is light, less dense than any kind of meat or fish. Grains are naturally bland and although seasoned by sauces and other additions need a stimulating wine with acidity and fresh or spicy fruit. The individual choice will depend very much on other elements in the dish, but generally lower tannin or plenty of masking fruit is required, as well as vigour and strength of flavour.

Vegetables lack protein and therefore require lower tannin and, depending on the style of cooking, less really crisp acidity in the wine. Oak can also overpower most vegetables and vegetable-based dishes unless a lot of dairy products are included. As vegetables need lightness, fruit and freshness, there are generally more suitable whites and rosés than reds, though classic Rieslings, Sauvignons and Chablis are to be avoided. Light fruity reds, such as Chinon or unoaked Merlot can work but Beaujolais and its like are too vigorous in fruit and acidity.

Vegetables generally have light, crisp textures needing light or medium-bodied wines. Many, like carrots, onions, peppers are sweet in taste and need a wine rich in fruit if not residual sugar, for example, Marsanne with root vegetables or Gewürztraminer with peppers.

Certain others, like tomatoes and spinach, are high in acid, and therefore need acidity in an accompanying wine—the fruitier kinds of Sauvignon Blanc would be suitable.

If serving a highly flavoured vegetable dish it is best to avoid very aromatic wines.

Stunning combinations of wine and cheese

Port and Stilton
French blue and Sauternes or similar fine dessert wine
Crottin de Chèvre and Sancerre
St Maure and Vouvray
Champagne and buffalo mozzarella
Meursault and Brie
Farmhouse Cheddar and sweet Jurançon
Hard English cheese, not Wensleydale, and St Émilion

The celebrated partnership of wine and *cheese* is not always very successful, hence the old wine-merchants' adage: 'Sell on cheese, buy on an apple.' It is not so much that cheese makes wine taste better, rather it prevents the taster from picking up faults.

Full fat, ripened cheeses coat the palate, making tasting difficult. The salty flavours and acidity of many cheeses—goats', blue, and Wensleydale for example—can positively clash with red wine and really need something sweet or fortified or intensely aromatic such as Sancerre and goats' cheese or port and Stilton. Mature and pungent cheeses are also difficult as their strength of flavour easily overpowers subtle tastes in wine. A traditional cheeseboard is a nightmare for there is no possibility of finding a wine to suit the usual combination of creamy, blue, hard and pungent cheeses so often presented. The best option is to serve a single cheese, or at least one type of cheese, with an appropriate wine. Failing that avoid blue, goat or any really pungent cheeses on a mixed board. Hard, nutty cheeses and waxy Gouda or Gruyère are the kindest to wine.

Aromatic or sweet white wines and rich reds like Pomerol or Australian Shiraz are often the best choice for the compromise route. As a general rule, the stronger the cheese, the more fruit and sugar needed in the wine. High acidity combined with fruit or sugar often helps. Avoid tannin with anything blue, creamy or tangy or with very mature cheese.

Adding a *sauce* with butter, cream, olive oil or egg yolks gives a dish more body. All these sauces are rich and therefore require acidity to cut the texture and bring out the flavour of the food. Herb butters, beurre blanc and butter-enriched bouillons are the lightest of these sauces: they need fruity, aromatic wines—cool climate flavours with crisp acidity, like Sancerre, Riesling Kabinett or Chablis. Hollandaise-type sauces need acidity with body, like Alsace or Sancerre. Cream sauces are more substantial than butter and match the dry bite of oak, in either white or red wine depending on the flavours.

A cream and shellfish sauce served with turbot might suit cooler style Australian or New Zealand Chardonnay, while cream and mushrooms served with chicken or guinea-fowl would need a medium-bodied red, a Pinot Noir or Rioja for example.

Oil-based sauces and dressings are used more and more not just for salads but for pasta, fish, meat and vegetables. Like all fats, oil is cloying but olive oil also has a very distinctive fruity flavour, and some natural acidity or bite, which varies with the type and origin of the oil. Generally wines which are dry and not too aromatic work best. Pasta with olive oil and herbs goes well with a medium-bodied Italian red like Barbera. Trendy roasted vegetables with extra virgin olive oil need softer wine as they are too sweet and fruity for classic levels of acidity and tannin. Different vegetables suit different flavours—aubergines with Zinfandel, root vegetables with Marsanne or Australian Chardonnay. Nut oils like walnut or hazel, especially with a warm salad, combine well with acidity and often a touch of sweetness, depending on the main ingredient. A rich and lightly aromatic Pinot Gris from Alsace is a good choice.

Soy sauce is salty and brings out and enhances other flavours.

Tannic wines or those with dominant oak tend to taste drier and more tannic with a dish containing soy. Light, crisp fruit flavours, aromatic whites, fruity rosés or light reds which are not too dry are the best choice. Wines with residual sugar as well as good acidity, are also successful as the salt-sugar effect is complementary. With barbeque marinades for steak, ribs or kebabs, the rich, 'sweet' fruit of Zinfandel or a luscious Shiraz is a good choice.

Oil enriches foods and lowers the acidity of anything combined with it. Think of the effect of blending oil into vinegar for a salad dressing. The effect on wine is similar—oil-rich dishes lower the freshness and liveliness of wine. Different oils have different flavours. Olive oil comes in a variety of strengths—ordinary oil used for cooking and different types of virgin oil used for salads, sauces and dressings. The stronger the flavour of the oil the more savoury and fruity the flavours needed from the wine.

Oak in Rioja, Italian and Portuguese reds and in New World Cabernet and Shiraz provides a dry bite which cuts through the richness of the oil. At the same time, the ripe fruit flavours enhance the taste. Acidity is needed in the white wines and generally not too aromatic fruit, which can simply taste too rich with the oil. Italian white wines, dry Australian Semillon, anything made with Malvasia or a sprightly Vinho Verde are all usually successful.

Hazelnut and walnut oils are quite strong in flavour and need rich flavours from the wine—again oak and non-aromatic tastes work best. Sesame oil is slightly lighter and can work well with richer, honeyed fruit flavours.

Vegetable purées are generally low in fat and vary in flavour between pungent (garlic), acid (sorrel), bitter (watercress) and sweet (red pepper). They all match fruity, light to medium-bodied wines, with soft tannins in the case of red. Sorrel works well with Sauvignon Blanc or New World Riesling, aubergine with rosé or a Syrah-based red, garlic with a light crisp white, a dry rosé or pink Champagne. Red pepper is best with New Zealand Sauvignon or a soft, rich red from southern Italy.

With *gravy* or *jus* the key is reduction. Simple meat juices have little effect on wine, neither does gravy unless contaminated by some form of flavour enhancer. In professional cooking, however, such sauces are usually heavily reduced to concentrate the flavours and enrich the consistency. Very intensely reduced sauces have a lot of caramel and even Bovrilly flavours which are tricky with wine as they can increase the effects of tannin and overpower subtle flavours. The answer is spicy new oak, sweetness and vigorous fruit. Reserva Rioja can work as can Syrah or Grenache-based wines, certain New World Cabernets or Bordeaux from a ripe, hot vintage.

Salsa, relishes, etc. and non-classic sauce/salad/chutney combi-nations can be very tricky with wine. Spices, vinegar, and sweet and sour flavours in general tend to dominate a dish, and usually provide a total contrast to the flavours. With light dishes, fresh, slightly neutral white wines are refreshing—New World Riesling has enough acidity and complementary citrus fruit flavours, and a slightly sweet Spätlese or Auslese can work well. With reds, try Beaujolais, Dolcetto or the fruitier kind of Zinfandel.

Pesto and *tapenade* are very pungent, southern Mediterranean flavours which need clean, dry fruit. Rosé or a light white like Pinot Grigio work well with a first course dish. More substantial dishes of pasta or lamb with tapenade are better with fruity substantial reds from the southern Rhône or Provence, or with a Shiraz or Garnacha.

Olives are both rich and salty with a positively meaty texture. Nibbled before a meal they go beautifully with fino sherry or a dry Provençale rosé. Olives in a sauce require more fruit and robust flavour from the wine than would otherwise be chosen.

Cooked *yoghurt*, in a korma for example, gives a creamy

consistency with mild acidity which is often helpful in bringing up flavours in wine as well as food. Raw yoghurt in a salad or sauce is more dominant. The acidity is quite high and needs corresponding zip from the wine. A light, very fresh white wine, Spanish or Italian, is good for yoghurt dips or salads like raita. Yoghurt dressings on fish or chicken are probably influenced more by the other flavours—usually herbs and spices—than directly by the yoghurt, but fresh fruity wines are generally best.

On the whole *herbs* add to the savoury flavours of a dish and create a more interesting accompaniment to wine. Many wines themselves have herbal notes which are complemented by the flavours in food.

The effect of a herb depends both on its strength of flavour and in the way it is used. For example, chicken cooked in stock with tarragon sprigs is quite mild, in fact the tarragon allows you to enjoy a more aromatic, interesting wine, whereas in kebabs marinated with rosemary, thyme and bay leaves, the herb flavours are much stronger and the wine needs to be more assertive, with primary fruit and plenty of vigour. A dish of tagliatelle with pesto is dominated entirely by the basil flavour and needs really assertive fruit with lively acidity; a vibrant red is usually most successful.

Bitter herbs have the most impact on wine. The strong flavours of rosemary and bay respond very well to young red wines and to the slightly sharp flavour of Italian reds in particular.

Sage can be problematic, especially if too much is used, as the flavour is pungent and all-pervading. Again Italian reds work, as does New World Merlot with a little oak or Portuguese reds. Lighter dishes of veal escalopes can be matched by white wines, nutty or not too aromatic in character.

Aromatic herbs like marjoram, oregano, parsley and thyme are good with Sauvignon-based whites or spicy, slightly earthy reds depending on the dish. Surprisingly, basil is often better with red wine than white, something with plenty of fruit, not too much oak and crisp acidity, though New World Riesling or Chardonnay, if not over-oaked, can work with fish or chicken combinations. Coriander, too, complements the fruit of the Riesling or dark, rich southern reds.

The aniseed flavours of fennel and, to a lesser extent, dill are good with full-bodied, non-aromatic southern white wines and with some of the new style whites of Greece and southern Italy when combined with fish. Pork and fennel works well with a light, slightly sharp red such as Barbera.

Mint, provided it is not in the form of vinegary mint sauce, is good with Cabernet, especially richly fruity Californian and Argentinian examples.

Spices have the reputation of being enemies of wine. Hot spices burn the palate and make tasting difficult or impossible. Most spices come from culinary traditions which are not part of a wine-drinking culture and seem to lack sympathy. However, there are many relatively strong spices in everyday use which blend readily with wine and in many cases the combination of highly-flavoured food and carefully chosen wine can be very satisfying.

Chilli and really hot spices will damage wine as the subtler flavours cannot be appreciated by a scorched palate. Tannin or oak in wine tends to be exaggerated by hot spices and the bitterness in each brought out, therefore reds need more careful choosing. Beaujolais works well with Chinese food, Dolcetto with spicy pepperoni or hot sausages, Chilean Merlot (not oaky) with spicy meatballs.

Hot peppers, large amounts of ginger, horseradish, cardamom and mustard are all potentially fiery and can numb the palate. Moderate amounts of heat do, however, stimulate the sense of taste and wines which emphasise primary fruit, possibly with some residual sugar and refreshing acidity, can work successfully. Aromatic grapes and simple direct flavours survive the onslaught of hot food and at the same time provide a refreshing contrast.

Aromatic spices such as cumin, coriander, cinnamon, saffron and lemon grass are easier with wine. Again they need aromatic wines with plenty of fruit and individual flavour.

Meat dishes with Middle Eastern spices go well with the fruity, earthy flavours of the Languedoc, southern Italian wines or Australian varietals without too much oak.

Saffron takes well to Vouvray or a full-bodied Chardonnay, while lemon grass and coriander have a citrus influence which is good with Sauvignon Blanc or Riesling. The choice between red and white, or indeed rosé, which can be an excellent option, will depend on the nature of the dish. Tannic, very mature or heavily oaked wines are generally better avoided.

Certain grape varieties work well—Sauvignon, Riesling, Gewürztraminer among the whites, Merlot, New World Pinot Noir and Grenache among the reds. Shiraz is also very good for anything based on pepper.

Problem ingredients

Food which combines a number of strong individual flavours can also be problematic with wine. More than one sauce, elaborate garnishes, spices and herbs can give so much taste and challenge that only the most direct wine flavours will work.

Too many different tastes or a number of strong contrasts will destroy most good wines. This can be a real problem with some of today's cross-cultural cooking which freely blends the spices and sauces of the Orient with robust Mediterranean and charcoal grilled dishes.

Wines with any complexity, subtlety or age will fight a losing battle with such an assault of food flavours. In general, culinary zeal or excess is a greater problem than individual ingredients. That said, there are a few notorious énfants terribles of the larder when it comes to combining wine and food. Such ingredients should be considered first when choosing an accompanying wine and are generally an indication to stay away from the finest botttles.

Globe artichokes and to a lesser extent *asparagus* tend to change the taste of wine due to the presence of an enzyme called cynarin. They blunt the freshness and acidity of wine and in some cases give a sickly sweet effect. Artichokes in a mixed salad, pasta etc go best with a clean, fresh, neutral white wine, or stick to water while eating the offenders! Asparagus is easier, especially if served with a rich hollandaise or other buttery sauce. Fumé Blanc can work rather well with a main dish which includes asparagus and cool fino sherry or dry Muscat is successful with a first course.

Much is made of the damaging effect of *tomatoes'* acidity but while it is not advisable to combine a really fine wine with tomato sauce or salad, the acidity of tomatoes is usually already balanced in the dish and provided the accompanying wine has plenty of fresh acidity and generous fruit it should not suffer. New Zealand Sauvignon Blanc, Beaujolais or Dolcetto are all good, while with a really rich, ripe tomato dish try something red, warm and spicy from southern Italy or Sicily.

Vinegar and wine are pretty obvious enemies and the ability to combine wine with a dressed salad depends very much on the quality of the dressing. Certainly the vinegar used should be mild wine vinegar or just possibly cider, in proportions of one part vinegar to four parts oil. Red wine vinegar is less sharp than white and the best is oak-aged like wine and mild, fruity and aromatic. Sherry vinegar is also good. Balsamic vinegar is extremely concentrated with a sweet-sour flavour that needs wines with a lot of fruit and crisp acidity to match its pungent tastes.

If you are serving a fine wine it is worth using wine rather than vinegar in the dressing which will give enough sharpness to the salad without damaging the wine.

Although Champagne and scrambled eggs may be the classic decadent breakfast, *eggs* are a very alkaline food which when cooked simply have little affinity with wine. Fried eggs are the worst, especially as the yolk remains soft and coats the palate to make tasting very difficult indeed. Omelettes are more wine-friendly, especially when filled with another more sympathetic flavour and cheese soufflés can be very flattering to better white wines, for example, white Burgundy to accompany a gruyère soufflé. Mayonnaise is another problem, as it is rich and cloying. Oaked Chardonnay is usually the best choice, or dry Australian Semillon or Graves, especially if the mayonnaise is lemony or herb flavoured.

The strong tastes of *smoked fish* such as kippers and smoked mackerel can be a real problem with wine as they are both pungent in flavour and oily in texture. Fino or New World Sauvignon Blanc stand the best chance. Smoked salmon, smoked trout and smoked eel are more subtle and actually form one of the great classic partnerships with fine Riesling Kabinett. Alsace Pinot Gris or Gewürztraminer or a Pouilly-Fumé are also con-tenders.

Two liquids together never seem that successful and on the whole chunkier *soups* work best. Garlicky Mediterranean seafood soup is good with a dry, not too aromatic white or a dry rosé, while seafood chowder works well with Pouilly-Fumé or New World Sauvignon. Dark onion, mushroom and lentil soup go well with a robust, simple red like Côte du Rhône, while min-estrone takes a full-bodied white or light, dry red. Cream soups, purées and consommés are often best with the classic glass of dry sherry-fino or amontillado depending on the flavours in the soup, though Rhine Riesling also works well.

The sweet-sharp-tangy effect of *chutney* is pretty devastating to wine. The best compromise is a really fruity, slightly jammy red such as Barossa Shiraz or Zinfandel. Reserva or even Gran Reserva Rioja can work if the chutney is not too aggressive. With *pickles* and *capers*, the gremlin here is once again the vinegar in which they are preserved. The effect on wine depends on how much of the ingredient is used. In a dish, the sharpness is usually offset by a fatty ingredient, such as capers with smoked salmon or the egg and oil of sauce tartare, but an accompanying wine still needs lots of fruit and aromatic spice as well as its own acidity to stand up to the impact. Sauvignon Blanc or Gewürztraminer have enough fruit and spice respectively; and light, fruity Italian reds are also highly successful.

Hot *chilli* burns the palate so that little else can be tasted. It clashes with the tannin in red wine, creating a harsh aggressive flavour which benefits neither food nor wine. Really fiery chilli needs only water or at most lager. Milder chillis, used in smaller quantities and offset by cream, olive oil or vegetable flavours can match wines with similarly assertive tastes. Fresh, aromatic white wines are refreshing and have enough fruit to stand up to the chilli flavour, while fruity, soft and spicy reds like Grenache, Merlot or Shiraz, provided they have not too much oak, are also very good.

Citrus flavours are mostly a problem in savoury dishes such as duck with orange, fish with lime or Chinese lemon chicken. Riesling has a great affinity with citrus tastes and Spätlese or Auslese is a classic with duck. For Oriental dishes try a New World version.

In sweet dishes citrus flavours, though not the actual fruit, are usually helpful as they balance the sweetness of the sweetmeat with the acidity of the wine, for example, botrytized Sémillon with lemon tart.

Sweet ingredients can also prove problematic. For dessert-friendly ideas see Chapter 12.

Icecream freezes the palate and neutralises tastebuds so is no friend to wine. Richer parfaits or frozen soufflés which have been properly softened before serving are slightly better. Ice-cream is not usually a pudding for wine, but if one is needed, try a sweet sparkling wine like Asti Spumante or a fortified Muscat.

Chocolate coats the palate with its fatty texture and makes it difficult to taste more subtle flavours. It is also intense in taste—dark chocolate is bitter and rich, milk chocolate creamy and very sweet. Dark chocolate puddings are best with sweet fortified wines, Banyuls from the south of France, tawny port or Australian liqueur Muscat. For a light chocolate mousse or soufflé, a sweet sparkling wine works well or the light, grapey Moscato d'Asti of Piedmont.

Coffee flavours in sauces, cakes or mousses present a similar problem to chocolate—the flavour is bitter, intended to close the palate at the end of a meal. With a really intense coffee flavour fortified wines survive best, otherwise serve a small brandy or liqueur.

Selecting wine for food is most focused in a restaurant setting when time is limited, costs high and food varied. As an opening gambit, a glass of house white wine ordered as an apéritif gives time to assess the list and is also a fair indication of the restaurant's wine skills: a crisp, fresh, appetising house wine is usually an indication of careful choosing and the list is sure to yield some good things which allow you to be adventurous. The quantity of wine required, and therefore the flexibililty to choose different wines, depends on the number of people. Two diners will drink a bottle or even two over a long, leisurely meal. Four will manage three bottles comfortably, and a party of six will easily get through four bottles. A larger number of people means a longer meal and consumption rises accordingly. Decide roughly on the amount you want to pay, perhaps economising with an initial wine to allow for something better later on.

After practical matters of quantity and price, and a general idea of whether it is a 'play it safe' or exciting wine list, the type of menu and cuisine will dictate the wine.

In *Oriental* restaurants go for light, fruity wines, possibly with residual sugar to offset the spices. If numbers permit two wines, start with a refreshing, light wine: Champagne, a north Italian varietal or even cold fino sherry. These go well with Chinese appetisers like wontons or other dumplings, and also with sushi, spicy pastries or tiny satays of chicken or seafood. Follow with something more aromatic or richer in taste. New World Sauvignon Blanc or Riesling from Germany or the New World is good with Thai cooking, Marsanne or Australian Chardonnay for milder, creamy curries and biryanis, Gewürztraminer for Szechuan food or a jammy, rich Barossa Shiraz for chilli with beef.

Italian restaurants usually feature their own wines which combine well with the food. Remember that in Italy pasta is a first course and the heavier, classic wines like Barolo or Riserva Chianti are meant for meat or game. Lighter wines with high acidity such as Barbera, Rosso Conero or Montepulciano d'Abruzzo are best for pastas with meat, cheese or a creamy sauce. Light, fresh, neutral Italian whites like Frascati or Pinot Grigio are a refreshing start which go well with antipasti, fried fish or shellfish. These delicate whites are also a good choice for a light escalope of chicken or veal.

Vegetable-based pasta with tomato, herb or olive oil-based sauces are best with the rich fruit flavours of the south and wines like Corvo or Salice Salentino while lighter meat dishes respond beautifully to the light, bitter fruit of north Italian reds from Valpolicello to Refosco.

In *classic French* restaurants the food is the ideal foil to the country's finest wines; however, a restaurant is not the best place to order a mature claret or Burgundy as there is rarely time to enjoy it unless you have planned and ordered in advance. St Émilion and Pomerol are the more approachable side of Bordeaux, and a Médoc from a lighter year can be very appealing with refined, carefully prepared food. Loire whites and the wines of Alsace provide excellent variety and the Rhône and south of France have individual reds of great character.

Much depends on the style of the cooking. Bold flavours and heavily reduced sauces need vigour and flavour so choose younger wines from warm vintages with new oak and spicy fruit, or try a New World alternative, which many French restaurants now offer. Bistro food is usually simple and rustic with lots of casseroles, herb and garlicky flavoured dishes. Again young, fruity and vigorous wines are needed: Beaujolais, Corbières or another regional choice is best.

Trendy eclectic menus such as *Mediterranean, Cal-Ital* or *Pacific Rim*, are challenging for wine and need fruity, aromatic assertive wines to stand up to the variety of ingredients and tastes. This type of cooking is not based on classic harmony and uniform flavour. Many dishes combine various strong flavours and contrasts on the same plate. Olive oil, spices, herbs and garlic are generously used, as are balsamic vinegar, sundried tomatoes and vegetables, relishes, salsas and chutneys of all kinds. New World fruit is the best accompaniment—wines with the richness and positive flavour of ripe grapes and new oak add to the vibrant tastes on the plate and hold their own at the same time.

Apart from the general style of the menu, individual food choices will affect wine in a restaurant. Two people eating together, one eating steak, the other scallops, is a difficult proposition. Make use of half bottles, possibly starting with a whole bottle of white which will suit both first courses and can be finished with the scallops, then choose a half of red for the steak.

If you have to choose only one wine for very different foods, a light red often goes well with fish, or at least does not clash, especially with sauced dishes. For larger numbers, different wines can be ordered to accompany different choices. Avoid too much variety by selecting a lighter option which may suit many of the first courses and can be drunk with lighter main dishes as well, followed by a more full-bodied wine for those eating game or heavier meats. If the wine choice has to be a compromise, avoid wines which are likely to clash with certain foods such as those with high tannin, a lot of oak or a particularly austere style.

Good choices of wine for restaurant meals

Champagne
Champagne with everything—perhaps not—but it is a versatile food wine for spicy food, rich mousses, cheese dishes and fish.

Rosé
Dry rosé is not a half-way choice; its fruit and acidity work beautifully with strong flavours and spice.

Fino sherry
This is a good apéritif which also suits seafood, spicy snacks, soups and deep-fried foods.

White Rhône
Full-bodied enough for meats or poultry, this also suits grilled fish or vegetable dishes.

Pinot Gris
Full-bodied, appetisingly spicy, this wine can suit a rich pâté, pork or poultry or a delicate fish.

Australian Marsanne
The round full character is especially good with spices and vegetables but has enough structure for meat dishes.

New World Pinot Noir
Highly versatile with many fish dishes, and is a good choice for meats and anything spicy.

Chinon
An excellent savoury choice which is flexible with food.

Mâcon-Villages
Easy to drink and non-assertive for fish and chicken.

Chilean Merlot
With its vibrant fruit, soft tannin and unobtrusive oak, this is a good choice for spices or light dishes.

Reserva Rioja
The combination of sweet fruit, spicy oak and soft tannin makes this wine versatile for poultry or meat.

5 WHITE WINES

Light dry white wines

These include a large range of fresh, light, vibrant wines with an emphasis on primary and fruit flavours. At one end of the flavour scale is Muscadet: tinglingly fresh, youthful, slightly yeasty in character; at the other lies Mosel or Rhine Riesling: brilliant, vibrant, aromatic with bracing acidity and intense, long-lasting fruit. In between is a whole range of wines which emphasise fruit and freshness with varying degrees of aroma and acidity. These include consciously young wines like Vinho Verde and some Grüner Veltliner; wines from certain grape varieties, notably those of Italy—Pinot Grigio, Soave, Verdicchio; light fruity wines which have benefited from modern vinification technology such as those of Rueda and Rías Baixas in Spain to the 'new' wines of Portugal, Italy and the south of France and finally, other German grape varieties and crossings, Austrian white wines and Silvaner and Pinot Blanc from Alsace.

The characteristics of the style are moderate alcohol, no oak, primary or fruit flavours and moderate to crisp acidity. Classically, these are products of cool climates, although modern winemaking can achieve a similar style in much warmer areas. The main stylistic variations are between the intensely aromatic and the more neutral styles, based on the grape variety. Levels of acidity also vary from the crisp Rieslings of the Mosel to the riper fruit style of Rueda and the fruity vins de pays of southern France, often with a little residual sugar to soften the wine. Most such wines emphasise clean, primary character, although good German Riesling can age well and become extremely complex.

These are the wines for simple, light foods or deliciously rich little dishes at the start of the meal. The delicacy of the wine can be overpowered by robust food, though a really intense Riesling can be a good match for rich, substantial flavours. The wines with higher acidity go well with the richest dishes, Riesling with sauced fish, Muscadet with mussels or oysters.

Clean, non-aromatic wines form a refreshing contrast to food with a lot of different flavours such as in hors d'oeuvres or antipasti and deep-fried fish and vegetables, while softer, fruitier styles are versatile apéritifs and can match buffet or spicy food.

Classic German Riesling with food

These wines are classified according to the ripeness of the grapes at harvest. The Kabinett and Spätlese catagories are considered here in relation to food. Wines in which the 'sweet' element is more definitive and richer, from Auslese up, are dealt with later. Fine German Riesling is based on the balance of fruit and acidity, a balance in which sweetness plays only a part, and which gives it its brilliant, lively character. Although light in body and alcohol—a fine Mosel Riesling may reach only seven per cent alcohol by volume—they have intensity of aroma and flavour.

Traditional food associations for Rhine Riesling include some of the richest dishes of pork and game and poultry like duck and goose. The combination of fruit and really crisp acidity offsets the fatty nature of the meat, in the same way as serving apple sauce with pork, while the intensity of flavour sustains the wine.

The acidity of such wines is a perfect match for rich sauces based on cream or butter. Mosel wines with their minerally, steely character are especially good with fish, while the wine of the Rhine itself, with a little extra roundness, matches poultry cooked in cream, and shellfish such as scallops which benefit from a richer wine. The light body of the wine is perfect for the most

Ten top matches for light, dry wines

Vinho Verde and avocado mousse
Riesling Kabinett and smoked salmon
Muscadet and mussels
Riesling Spätlese and spicy vegetable fritters
Soave and goujons of fish
Verdicchio with escalopes of chicken
Nahe or Pfalz Riesling Spätlese with Chinese wontons
Silvaner and leek quiche
Pinot Grigio and antipasti
Pinot Blanc with warm chicken salad

delicate fish while its brilliant acidity leaves a clean, refreshing finish no matter how rich the sauce. This combination of lightness and crispness works well with warm salads, especially those of chicken liver, game or shellfish, with certain pâtés and egg and cream pastries. They make a light, yet bracing start to a meal.

The fruit character together with the residual sugar is a classic for smoked salmon or trout, bringing out the sweet, smoked flavours while cutting through the oiliness of the fish. The same elements also work with spicy food, with mustard on fish or the intense flavours of Chinese or Thai cuisine. The fruit and sweetness bring out the flavours while the acidity is refreshing. Spiced vegetables, vegetable fritters or pastries are also successfully matched by the lightness and intensity of Riesling.

Medium-bodied dry white wines

This category includes wines made from some of the best known aromatic grape varieties, varieties which express the particular character of the grape without obvious oak, usually none at all.

The assertive fruit is offset by moderate to high acidity and extra body from ripeness, alcohol and extract.

The *Sauvignon Blanc* of the Loire is a classic, cool climate aromatic style, especially in the minerally, steely examples from Sancerre and Pouilly Fumé. This is a grape variety of big personality which keeps its pronounced, slightly wild aromas and green gooseberry fruit character no matter where it is grown. In New Zealand it makes one of the great varietal wines: bold and assertive, full of lime, green pepper and elderflower aromas which follow on to the taste. Chile also makes clean, varietal Sauvignon, lower in acidity than the classic style and generally lighter in intensity than the wines of New Zealand. The same style appears in many new winemaking areas, including southern regions of Europe where it imparts freshness to local grape varieties.

Bordeaux Blanc is another medium-bodied dry white made from all, or mostly, Sauvignon Blanc, sometimes with the extra roundness of Sémillon. The warmer region gives a softer style than the Loire.

Chenin Blanc, also from the Loire, is probably most associated with sweet wines but is also responsible for long-lived dry Vouvrays, the rare and elegant wines of Savennières and a host of lesser whites which are increasingly well made, aromatic and dry.

Alsace's principal white grape varieties are dry and strong, from the exotically perfumed, spicy *Gewürztraminer* to rich, subtle *Pinot Gris. Riesling* of Alsace is also most properly described as medium-bodied due to its alcohol levels which are higher than those from across the Rhine, and so too are the Rieslings of Australia, California and New Zealand.

The main distinction in style, apart from the characteristics of the individual grape varieties, is between varietal, fruit-led wines such as New Zealand Sauvignon Blanc, and those which express more the character of the region: Sancerre or Alsace Pinot Gris for example. Such wines can come from cool or relatively warm climates which also influence the ultimate style. In many years the Loire is an almost marginal area for viticulture and the wines are always characterised by steely, crisp acidity and grassy, green fruit flavours. Alsace is warmer and drier and the wines are typically dry and powerful.

Although they emphasise primary aromas and flavours, the individual grape variety, the concept of terroir and the age of the wine add complexity and the ability to match rich and complex dishes. Loire Chenin can age for a long time and Vouvray is usually most attractive with seven or eight years' ageing to expand its richer flavours and subdue the bracing acidity of the Chenin Blanc.

All these wines have a positive character of their own and are good accompaniments to strongly flavoured, rich and complex dishes. The wines' varied flavours: aromatic, spicy, vibrant, honeyed, steely or fruity, are especially good with herbs, sauces, smoked or spicy flavours and intense ingredients such as goats' cheese. Loire Chenin in particular is very good with rich mousselines of fish and shellfish with delicate sauces. The assertive, aromatic fruit of Sancerre is perfect with tangy, strong goats' cheeses or herb-flavoured river fish. Gewürztraminer matches spices, especially Chinese or Middle Eastern food; while the more direct flavours of the New World Sauvignon go with olive oil and herb dressings for fish or chicken, complex salads of cheese, vegetables and smoked foods and spicy Thai marinades.

As these wines have assertive flavours of their own they are the best choice for most strongly flavoured dishes. The absence of oak means that they work well with spices and vegetables, but are generally better with lighter sauces based on butter, reduction or perhaps olive oil than a very rich cream. Most Sauvignons have enough body for light meats such as chicken or veal, while a Pinot Gris is excellent with meaty fish or relatively strong meats like quail; it is especially successful with spices. The lighter, fruitier wines are excellent at a summer lunch or as an apéritif which can carry on to the first course. Sancerre, white Bordeaux, Chablis are all good first course wines for dinner, really stimulating the palate for the food and wine to follow. Varietal Sauvignon Blanc in particular is a versatile choice for a spicy buffet or seafood meal and such aromatic whites are often the best choice for flavoursome restaurant food.

Classic Sancerre with food

Sancerre is very much a terroir wine. The hill on which the vineyards lie has a number of different soil types and exposures which produce wines of different character, from the fruity and elegant to powerful, flinty and minerally wines which really need to be drunk with shellfish or a tangy crottin salad to bring out their best. Some producers blend the wines from different vineyards to produce their definitive Sancerre: aromatic and slightly wild, crisp and assertive with clean gooseberry fruit tinged with flint, a firm, steely structure and a long finish. Others produce individual wines to express the character of a particular vineyard. These are variously powerful, more full-bodied or highly aromatic in character.

Sancerre is a wine for food. In spite of its intense fruit the acidity sharpens the palate so much that more than one glass is hard to drink. It is a natural partner to the local cheeses, the river fish like perch or *sandre* and the beurre blanc for which the region is famous.

It is also good with smoked food, fish or poultry although because of the high acidity, hot spices are better avoided.

Well-made light sauces, especially flavoured with herbs, match the aromatic fruit of the wine very well, as do mixed fish dishes combining sea, river and shellfish in a flavoursome sauce.

Ten top matches for medium-bodied white wines

Sancerre and grilled crottin salad
Pouilly Fumé with salmon and herb-flavoured beurre blanc
Jurançon sec and roasted vegetable salad
Chablis and oysters
Tokay Pinot Gris with honey-glazed quail
Australian Riesling and spiced tiger prawns
Gewürztraminer and Peking duck
Dry Vouvray and mousseline of fish and shellfish
Chilean Sauvignon Blanc and tomato, avocado and
    mozzarella salad
New Zealand Marlborough Sauvignon and stir-fried
    chicken with Thai spices

Full-bodied dry white wines

The most full-bodied white wines are those which come from
warm or hot regions and have the extra structure and complexity
of oak and oak ageing. Even when young the complex flavours of
the grape emerge, combined with the effects of oak maturation.

The group includes the classic white wines of Burgundy and
Graves, oak-aged Chardonnay from many parts of the world, the
rich full-bodied wines of the Rhône and Southern France as well
as Semillon and Marsanne wines from Australia and the oaked
Fumé Blanc of California.

The style comes from the ripeness of the fruit, the full body
and higher alcohol of a hotter region—a more southern area of
France or a New World country—and from the use of oak. Oak
not only contributes specific characteristics of wood, it begins a
maturation process during which the wine develops body and
complexity.

Chardonnay is the grape most associated with oak ageing and this type of wine. Classic white Burgundy is made to suppress some of the primary fruit character through the slight oxidation given by racking and barrel ageing, in order to gain complex tertiary qualities of oak and age. Such handling is not necessarily confined to Burgundy and is quite different to the fruit driven wines made by the more automated techniques of modern winemakers. Varietal Chardonnay puts the emphasis on ripe fruit character; descriptions like pineapple, peach, honeydew melon spring to mind, along with toasted, vanilla oak flavours from the barrels. This comes from ripe fruit, the use of oak for specific flavours rather than maturation, and from controlled handling.

Other full-bodied white wines come from hot areas like the southern Rhône where high alcohol and only moderate levels of acidity produce full, round, non-aromatic wines.

Australian Semillon and Marsanne are also full-bodied, rich wines with ripe fruit flavours balanced by citrus-like acidity and often spicy oak flavours. Oak aged Sauvignon, in Graves or the New World, also develops oily fullness and a rounder texture through moderate barrel ageing.

When considering food oak is the most significant part of these wines. Barrel-fermentation and oak ageing add structure and body to wine which then needs more substance and texture from accompanying foods. The wines are simply more powerful and likely to overpower delicate ingredients or dishes. Oak is also drying and stimulating to the palate and works well with protein-rich foods and creamy, generous sauces as well as richer cooking methods like roasting or braising.

The way oak affects wine has only been studied and understood in the last twenty or thirty years. Originally wooden barrels were simply a convenient vessel for containing wine during making and storing. But barrels also introduce strong flavours, of the wood itself and also of the way in which a barrel is made:

Ten top matches for full-bodied white wines

New Zealand Chardonnay with fish pie
Puligny-Montrachet and lobster with truffle
Meursault with turbot and shellfish sauce
Chilean Chardonnay with pasta carbonara
Australian Marsanne with celeriac gratin
White Châteauneuf-du-Pape with grilled salmon teriyaki
White Rioja (traditionally oaked) with braised squid
Dry white Graves with brill in mussel and saffron sauce
Premier Cru Chablis with cheese and mushroom soufflé
Australian dry Semillon with pork fillet in cream and
    cumin

essentially, the heat applied to bend the staves and the degree of burning used on the inside of the eventual barrel dictates the degree of flavour from mildly toasty to caramelised and smoky.

These oak flavours go well with highly flavoured food, especially dishes which have been browned or coloured themselves in the cooking process. It is not good with spicy food, especially hot spices, as the dryness of the oak can have an effect similar to tannin. However, really ripe Australian Chardonnay is successful with mild curries cooked in coconut milk.

The dry bite of oak generally needs protein though certain root vegetables can work well with the more fruit-driven Chardonnays. Oak is especially good with dense, strongly flavoured sauces and braised dishes and the richest pastas.

Dominant, oaky flavours need very robust food indeed: barbecued fish or poultry, richly sauced lobster or creamy chicken pie; more subtle oak matches refined flavours of carefully made sauces and really simple foods like roasted farm chicken or simply cooked lobster.

Semillon and Marsanne are highly versatile; they may or may not have oak influence which is in any case more subdued than with most Chardonnays, and can match even spicy food like curries, rice dishes and stir-fries. They also work with vegetables and vegetarian foods like tofu and noodles. The gentler, less aromatic character of southern white wines, typically white Châteauneuf-du-Pape, is excellent with grilled fish or a rich garlicky fish casserole.

Classic white Burgundy

White Burgundy is characterised by full body and power, by a creamy, buttery mouthfeel and subtly integrated oak combined with varying degrees of maturation in a life which can span ten or more years. Direct fruit character is harder to describe as the Chardonnay is a grape variety which takes on different characters according to its handling, and most Burgundian producers are looking for complexity and age rather than fruit. Apples, melons, fresh peaches are typical aroma and palate descriptions along with minerally, spicy and buttery flavours.

The unique quality of fine Burgundy is its depth and intensity—this is not directly assertive or immediate but a huge palate of flavour which emerges gradually from the glass and lingers long in the mouth. The structure of the wine makes it the classic partner to well-textured fish like turbot with a classic sauce, boiled or grilled lobster or a fine Dover sole with a shellfish sauce. It is also perfect with simply roasted chicken, in fact possibly at its best, as the sheer power of Burgundy can be too much for many fish-based dishes. A farm chicken roasted in butter with some delicate herbs like tarragon is a perfect partner to such a complex wine.

White Burgundy is also good with anything creamy, including a humble fish pie. It goes well with lighter meats cooked with cream or a cream sauce and can be a fascinating partner for truffle risotto. Meursault and Chablis are good with cheese, especially soft-rinded cheeses like Brie which often clash with red wine. The main foods to avoid are highly spiced dishes, because of the oak in the wine, and the finer the Burgundy the more subtle the food should be to allow the complexity of the wine to show through.

Light-bodied fruity reds and rosés

The lively acidity and fresh fruit of the lightest red and rosé wines make them immensely versatile with food, especially as they lack the oak and tannin which can clash with certain ingredients. Modern winemaking in general puts more emphasis on fruit, and tannin levels are lower than in the past. Fruit is riper, gentler vinification techniques are used and periods of maceration are shorter. Fruity, low tannin styles come from vins de pays and AC wines of the Midi and the unoaked varietals of the New World, though the latter are usually more fruit-driven and richer in fruit than the light red wines of Europe.

Apart from winemaking, climate helps to produce lighter styles of red, typified by those of Alsace, Germany, Austria and the Loire Valley, where moderate temperatures give high acidity and light red fruit character.

The lack of tannin is a significant element in these wines, enabling them to match low protein foods from couscous to sandwiches, hot spices, fish and lighter textures. Immediate primary fruit flavours match strong aromatic foods and seasonings with the complex taste of a number of different ingredients while the acidity offsets rich, fatty elements.

Although generally versatile, there are a number of stylistic differences which influence the way in which these wines match food, mainly due to the character of the fruit and the way it is expressed. Beaujolais, made from the Gamay grape, most young wines and simple varietals, are fruit-led, vibrant and immediate in style. They match the vigorous, robust flavours of sausages, pizza and highly flavoured pasta. Light Italian reds have a slightly bitter cherry twist in the fruit, typified by Valpolicella or Refosco, for example, which is especially good with rich meats, offal, cooked cheese dishes and intense tomato sauces.

The intensity of fruit is generally less good with vegetable-based dishes—here rosés really come into their own. Really ripe fruity styles are especially useful with salty or smoked flavours. Rosé can be dry and subtle, such as those of Provence and parts of Spain, or more fruity, such as those of the Languedoc or the New World. Though often trivialised, a good rosé is a wonderful start to a summer meal and goes well with garlicky dips, pâtés or well-flavoured salads.

Loire reds are quite different again, especially Chinon and Bourgueil made from the Cabernet Franc grape. Even in a ripe vintage the wines have a stalky, savoury quality which is good with classic sauces and cooking based on stocks and dairy produce. Served slightly cool they are excellent with carefully cooked fish.

Classic Beaujolais with food

Beaujolais is the quintessential light, fruity red wine which makes the greatest virtue out of youth and freshness. It is largely produced by a form of carbonic maceration, a special type of vinification at a high temperature for a short period in a sealed environment which releases colour and fruit, but little or no tannin. Wines so produced have a characteristic aroma and intensely fruity character. The youngest wines of other regions, made for early drinking rather than further development, are also light and fruity. These include *vino joven* from Spain, Chianti Normale and some AC Bordeaux.

The lively fruit of simple young Beaujolais, *vin de l'année*, gives way to suave, velvety though extremely fruity flavours in the

Top ten matches for light fruity reds

Beaujolais and salami
Chilean Merlot (unoaked) and spicy chicken wings
Rosé de Provence and aubergine purée
Grenache rosé and rabbit terrine
Chianti Normale and pasta alla Matriciana
Fleurie and grilled poussin
Chinon with roasted cod
Valpolicella and char-grilled squid
Corbières (fruity, unoaked style) with spicy couscous
Spätburgunder with baked Kassler

wines of the *cru* villages such as Fleurie or Chiroubles.

Traditionally made wines, now quite rare, especially those of Juliénas or Moulin à Vent, have more structure, but the same intense fruit quality.

These are great food wines. After all Beaujolais is the 'local' wine of Lyon, often called the capital of French gastronomy, home to some of France's finest restaurants and most famous chefs. Imaginative cooking with strong flavours and many different tastes suits the direct fruit and lively acidity of a good Beaujolais. The wine refreshes the palate, and the elegant fruit, especially in the *cru* and village wines, stands up to rich complex cooking.

As the emphasis is on fruit and freshness, Beaujolais is best served cool, even chilled, in summer and with light food. At its simplest level, it is a super picnic wine to go with chunky pâtés and terrines, cold cuts and salamis, even hearty sandwiches of meat or cheese. It does not go well though with vegetable dishes unless cheese or mushrooms dominate; somehow, the intense fruit suits meaty or smoky flavours rather than the sweeter aromatic qualities of most vegetables.

The vigorous fruit also matches spicy food and the sweet-spicy-salty flavours of Chinese cooking, as well as barbecue kebabs or sausages. The more subtle *cru* wines are good with chicken and lighter meats and with very intense sauces.

Medium-bodied red wines

A large and diverse range of red wines is described as medium-bodied. Certain wines can be closer to full-bodied depending on the year and the maker, especially Australian Shiraz and the wines of the southern Rhône villages. All have more complexity than simple fruit styles with added notes of spice and elegance, and have added structure from moderate amounts of tannin and oak.

The great classic of such wines is red Burgundy, perhaps the most supremely elegant of red wines. Made from the Pinot Noir grape it is a wine of long, memorable flavour. Oak and tannin are present, but as a finely balanced part of an elegant structure. The natural acidity and spicy, earthy flavours which typify Pinot Noir make it a good match for rich, complex food; think of the gastronomy of Burgundy with its rich, long-simmered casseroles, its game and dark, intensely reduced wine sauces.

Pinot Noir from other countries is also a natural food wine, the usually more fruit-pronounced style of California or New Zealand can be a stunning partner to spicy, exotic flavours.

The wines of the southern Rhône, along with the more structured wines from Languedoc Roussillon, also emphasise complex fruit flavours, often with peppery and earthy tones, characteristic of the grape variety—especially the Syrah and Mourvèdre—and the environment, with moderate structure and well-ripened, hot climate fruit which adds richness of flavour.

Many of the red wines of central and southern Spain, for example, from Navarra and the Duero Valley, and from Portugal,

e medium-bodied but with more oak—sweet and spicy in the
se of Spain, smoky and dry from Portugal.

Italy's rossos, the stuff of everyday drinking with plates of pasta
nd polenta, are strangely aromatic, though not fruity in bouquet
nd with a bitter twist to sharpen the palate. Further south they
ecome riper, with spicy, dried fruit flavours from the Mediterra-
ean sun which match the vibrant vegetable and olive oil-based
uisine.

Many New World wines, especially Merlots, Shiraz and
infandel, are at the fuller end of medium-bodied. Fruit-driven
nd high in alcohol, they emphasise varietal character and new
ak flavours, and are concentrated and structured with well
asked tannins.

The style varies with the heat of the climate, from relatively
ool Burgundy and New Zealand fruit to the rich, ripe flavours of
e Barossa Valley or the Mediterranean. Certain grape varieties
ave marked character which shows through regional and indi-
dual variations; the fragrant, heady, elegance of Pinot Noir, the
eppery kick of the Syrah, the fleshy hedonistic charm of Merlot
nd the rich sweet fruit of Zinfandel.

The type of winemaking in general and the amount of oak in
articular, also influence the character of the wine. The strong
ew oak influences of Spain and the New World add sweet spice
avours mixed with toffee and caramel tones which are quite
sertive. In France, oak is more a structural influence providing
ice and smoke flavours which are generally more integrated into
e wine.

The appetising dry wines of Portugal and Italy are more austere
anks to high acidity or bitterness in the grape variety, tradi-
onal long maceration and old oak-ageing. More fruit-driven
yles have riper fruit flavours and a more rounded, softer bal-
ce.

Most of these wines have enough structure and tannin to

benefit from protein foods, red meat and quite rich cooking methods. The extra complexity of the wine suits integrated flavours and well-flavoured sauces. Individual combinations depend on the grape variety, the general austerity of the wine and its origin. The more reserved, drier wines, especially those of Italy and Portugal, need rich food, ingredients like pork or braised meat, rich sauces and fatty dishes with beans and olive oil, as well as vigorous flavours of garlic and herbs. Riper fruit and the mellow effects of new oak, give a rich softness which matches lighter meats like chicken and turkey and smoked foods like ham and generally suit less rich styles of cooking.

Pinot Noir has a special affinity with game and the spicy, strong flavours of heavily reduced sauces and spices. Shiraz goes with anything peppery and many other hot spices, as well as robust cuts of meat, especially beef. Depending on the amount of oak, Merlot matches roast or sauced meat dishes, pastas with meat and richer vegetable dishes while Zinfandel works with the barbecue flavours of slightly sweet marinades and charcoal.

Classic Burgundy with food

At its best, red Burgundy is a supremely complex wine with layer of sumptuous flavour, an elegant structure and heady concentration. Individual wines have subtle differences but in general, the wines of the Côte de Beaune have the greatest finesse, fragrance and delicacy, while the wines of the Côte de Nuits have a more spicy intensity mixed with heady fruit scents and flavour. Some Burgundy is extremely light in tone but can be very intense and concentrated in taste.

The relatively high acidity of Pinot Noir combined with subdued, well integrated tannins and oak, make Burgundy a good choice for classic dishes and subtle, rich sauces. The concen tration of flavour in the best wines can match the strong tastes o

Top ten matches for medium-bodied reds

Mature (eight–ten year old) Premier Cru Côte de Nuits
and roast pheasant

Young red Burgundy, village wine, and wild mushroom
ragoût

Côte de Beaune Premier Cru and monkfish cooked in
red wine

Californian Pinot Noir (Carneros) and spice-crusted
salmon

Barbera d'Alba and lasagne

Salice Salentino Rosso and stuffed aubergine

Zinfandel and barbecued ribs

Dâo and pigeon

Barossa Shiraz and Szechuan beef

Red Côtes de Provence and saddle of rabbit

game, especially pheasant or wild duck and dark, long-simmered
casseroles of beef. The spice makes the wine refreshing with such
rich tastes and complements the complexity of the food.

The light elegant balance, which is the other side of Burgundy's
character, means that it can match chicken and even a meatier
fish like monkfish. As the emphasis in the wine is on depth of
flavour, balance and elegance rather than power and structure, the
way the food is cooked, especially the sauce, is very important.
Smaller dishes like mushroom pastries or risotto can work as well
as game if the flavour is sufficiently fine.

Burgundy can also work well with cheese, though not perhaps
the strongest of local varieties, unless the wine is very young and
simple. The spice goes well with mature hard cheeses and with
milder full fat varieties like Chaumes.

Full-bodied red wines

The common characteristic of all the great, long-lived, classic red is their complexity. The taste of such wines demands attention and develops constantly into a peacock's tail of flavours and nuances. The food needs careful consideration as it adds yet another dimension and should enhance the complete experience.

These wines include the best châteaux of the Médoc, Graves, Pomerol and St Émilion along with top Cabernet Sauvignon from other areas; the monumental reds of the Northern Rhône, the brooding Reservas of Spain and Italy, the top Shiraz of Australia and the Zinfandel of California. Such wines start out life with tannin and the ability to develop into a multi-dimensional maturity over five, ten, twenty or more years. They have concentration of fruit and flavour from the natural environment or terroir, and from the winemaking which is intended to nurture the best.

These are, above all, terroir wines; stylistic variation comes from the different origins, which in turn affect the grape variety and the intention of the winemaker. Age is another very important factor, and the character and ability of such wines to match certain foods change as they mature. A vigorous five-year-old Haut Médoc is well suited to dense sauces and strong aromatic flavours in a dish such as lamb with wild mushrooms or duck with sage. Ten years later the refined flavours of roast lamb would be more appropriate to the greater complexity but less vigorous structure of the older wine. All such full-bodied red wines need meat, or certain types of cheese, to offset the tannin and structure.

The wines of the Haut Médoc are extremely long-lived, complex and always a touch austere. They are wines which stimulate the palate and intrigue the mind. Pomerol and St Émilion are more sensuous, richer yet equally complex. In general the richer

Ten top matches for full-bodied reds

Pauillac and roast lamb
Hermitage and ribs of beef
Gran Reserva Rioja and pheasant
Barolo and game casserole
Chianti Riserva and stuffed pigeon
Taurasi Riserva and papardelle with hare
Victoria Shiraz and pepper steak
Zinfandel (such as Ridge or Ravenswood) and smoked
  lamb
Pomerol and quail and mushrooms
Grand Cru St Émilion and fillet of beef and shallot

wines are at their best with the leaner flesh of beef and wild meats while the Médoc suits duck and lamb.

Rioja Reserva and the top wines of Ribero del Duero have a lot of strength of flavour: dry, but without the austerity of the Médoc they match game and richer poultry dishes as well as meat. The Rhône and the New World's top Cabernet, Shiraz and Zinfandel are wines of power and concentration. They need vigorous food—game like venison, large cuts of beef and grilled steaks as well as wine-rich casseroles of beef or game. Italy's Barolo, Chianti and Carmignano Riserva and other aged Sangiovese wines are especially good with flavoursome meats and dishes and with robust cooking methods like braising.

Classic wines of Northern Italy

This category includes the best reds of Piedmont—Barolo and Barbaresco, which are made from the Nebbiolo grape; the Tuscan reds—both traditional Riserva Chianti, Carmignano, Brunello di Montalcino and Vino Nobile de Montepulciano, which are made from the Sangiovese grape; and the Super Tuscans of modern winemaking based on Sangiovese, Cabernet Sauvignon or a mixture of the two. Finally, Amarone of the Veneto is one of Italy's great full-bodied wines. Mature examples of such wines are unique and wonderfully complex and, with the possible exception of Amarone, are real food wines which only open out and reveal their true qualities with the right company.

Barolo and Barbaresco are characterised by high tannin, acidity, extract and alcohol and very full body. They are fragrant wines with layers of aroma which are always slightly elusive of description. Words like tar, cigars and smoke all spring to mind though none fully describe the experience. The dryness of the wines is wonderful with richly cooked meat. Long simmered, wine-rich beef casseroles, venison or wild duck bring out all the complexity of the wine which gives a dry bite of contrast to the rich food.

Riserva Chianti shows well with a simple steak, or any rare beef, but its inherent dryness and austerity also suit game such as pigeon, wild duck or venison. Wines in which the Cabernet Sauvignon dominates can have a very big structure which needs lots of protein and texture—again rare meat and game, and the enriching effects of sauces. A leg of autumn lamb cooked with herbs and garlic is also a fine accompaniment to the biggest wines of Tuscany.

Amarone is a very special wine whose character comes from the drying of the grapes prior to fermentation. This gives a very rich style, high in alcohol and tremendously intense in spice and ripe, almost dried fruit flavours. Styles vary in intensity and the 'lighter' versions can be drunk with main courses, perhaps a magret of duck with a good sauce, or a roast pigeon. The more intense kind really belong after dinner with cheese, especially Parmesan or nuts as the true *vino de meditazione.*

7 SPARKLING, SWEET, SHERRY AND PORT

Champagne and sparkling wines

The food occasions most associated with Champagne are weddings, romantic picnics, or long, late decadent breakfasts, when it is more a question of mood than food and wine.

Yet sparkling wine has a number of positive advantages for serving with food and can match many dishes which are tricky with still, dry wines. A sparkling wine is always something of a treat and is an ideal way to begin a meal or to enhance a party.

All sparkling wines are refreshing and appetising to the palate. Champagne has wonderfully crisp acidity together with a long, complex taste. Crémant and regional sparkling wines usually have a slightly softer edge and a less persistent mousse while Cava from northern Spain is very dry and clean in flavour. New World sparkling wines have more emphasis on fruit, and often a higher *dosage* than dry Champagne which makes them softer and richer. Moscatos, like Asti Spumante, are simple and sweet, great fun on a summer day, with bowls of strawberries and cream.

The refreshing quality of dry sparkling wines is excellent with rich food and also with hot spices: try an inexpensive, well-made sparkling wine with a Chinese meal for a good combination of flavours. Food which is very rich, yet light in texture—a mousseline of fish, some soufflés, a very rich pâté—will also respond well to sparkling wine.

The taste of Champagne is highly complex. In style it varies from very light and elegant to really full. In all fine Champagnes there is great length of flavour in the finish which allows it to show well against intensely flavoured food such as sushi, spicy Thai dishes, smoked fish and strong cheeses, especially goats'

Ten top matches for Champagne and sparkling wines

Rich Champagne (off-dry) with Thai green chicken curry
Non-vintage Champagne with sushi
Vintage pink Champagne with pheasant and truffles
Californian sparkling wine with chicken and mango salad
Cava with garlic dip
Champagne with oysters
Sekt with kedgeree
Australian sparkling wine with Chinese prawns
Asti Spumante with strawberry cheesecake
Champagne (full-bodied) with buffalo mozzarella and
    aubergine salad

cheese. The more full-bodied styles work with richly cooked
poultry and fine pink Champagne can be wonderful with game.

Vouvray Mousseux is a very good food wine due to the acidity
of the Chenin Blanc. The mousse tends to be full and creamy in
well-made examples and the wine beautifully balanced. It
matches rich dishes such as pâtés and shellfish mousse, as well as
strong, creamy cheeses.

New World sparkling wines are very good with spicy food
where the fruit and softer style balance the hot flavours. They can
also work well with savoury dishes which incorporate fruit,
something simple like melon and ham, or an exotic combination
of fruit, meat and spices.

Sweet wines

Some of the world's greatest wines are sweet. These are special
wines, many are rare, and all create excitement at the end of a
meal. However, matching two sweet tastes is more difficult than
combining a dry wine and a savoury dish.

Matching Food and Wine

Wine takes its sweetness from very ripe grapes, or at least from grape sugar, and is balanced by refreshing acidity which prevents the lusciousness from cloying and allows the wine to age and develop. Sweet food, on the other hand, is usually based on pure sugar, frequently with the added richness of cream and butter, for which the natural sweetness of wine is no match. The best desserts to serve with sweet wines are simple pastries and puddings while those based on orchard fruits and nuts are especially successful. Very rich, creamy cakes, mousses and creams with added liqueurs and elaborate confectionery are to be avoided.

Sweet wines can be successfully matched with certain savoury foods where they balance richness or complement salty flavours. Examples are the classic combinations of Sauternes and foie gras, or of sweet wine and blue cheese where the sharp, salty, tangy cheese is beautifully enlivened by the sweet fruit of the wine. Smoked and other salty foods also work well with sweet wines. Spicy food can also benefit from moderate sweetness as it complements the intensity of flavour and soothes the palate.

The style of a sweet wine varies according to its region, grape variety and wine-making. The finest are made from late-harvested, super-ripe grapes individually selected at just the right stage of maturity. Sauternes and Barsac in the south of the Graves are produced from late harvested Sémillon grapes, infected with *botrytis cinerea* or noble rot which further concentrates the sugars and adds to the complexity of the wine. They are intensely rich, warm and memorable wines, the best of which are magnificently long and complex in flavour.

Top Sauternes is extremely complex and luscious and is probably best combined with nuts or nutty puddings, blue cheese or a rich pâté, or, if you can find them, perfectly ripe pears or peaches. The less intense wines and those from satellite regions are good with simpler puddings including those based on custard, caramel or pastry. They also work with mature cheese, especially well-aged, nutty Cheddar.

Ten top matches for sweet wines

Muscat de Frontignan and baklava
Coteaux du Layon and pear tart
Sauternes and Roquefort
Rutherglen liqueur Muscat and chocolate biscuit cake
Jurançon Moelleux with pear and walnut tart
Banyuls and chocolate cake
Monbazillac and bread and butter pudding
New Zealand (Nelson district) late-harvest Riesling
    and lemon tart
Vouvray Moelleux and St Maure goats' cheese
Muscat de St Jean-de-Minervois and mature farmhouse
    Cheddar cheese

The Rhine produces a similar style from Riesling grapes in its
Beerenauslese and Trockenbeerenauslese wines made in excep-
tional years. These are lower in alcohol than Sauternes, often only
seven or eight per cent by volume, with clean acidity cutting
through the intense sweetness and the ability to age almost
indefinitely.

The sweet wines of the Loire, from the Côteaux du Layon and
especially Quarts-de-Chaumes and Bonnezeaux, and from
Vouvray, are made from the Chenin Blanc grape, harvested late in
suitable years. They may or may not be infected with *botrytis*
which is more common in Layon than further east. These wines
tend to have more fruit and maintain high acidity throughout
their life, which can be as much as fifty years.

Loire and Rhine wines usually have a more fruity character
which complements fruit pastries, fools and cakes, as well as
strong cheeses, especially goats' cheese.

Late-harvested wines from New World regions include Riesling, from California and New Zealand and Semillon from Australia. Rich, moderate to high in alcohol and intensely fruity they are particularly good with citrus flavoured puddings, lemon tart or orange cream, or with compotes of fresh fruit.

Some sweet wines are produced by fortification—stopping fermentation by the addition of alcohol before all the sugar has been fermented out. These include the *vins doux naturels* from the south of France made from the Muscat grape or, in the case of Banyuls, from the Grenache.

Specialities from outside France, both fortified and unfortified, include the liqueur Muscats of Australia and Hungarian Tokay and Italian Vin Santo, both of which are historic styles of sweet wine, aged in a deliberately oxidative environment which forms part of their character. The additional alcohol means that the stronger wine can match more intense, often alcohol-influenced food such as Christmas pudding and mince pies, as well as ingredients like chocolate.

Sherry and port

Most fortified wines are rather too strong to drink throughout a meal, the exception being fino sherry which goes down very well with shrimps and sunshine. However, at the first or last course, sherry or port respectively can make an interesting combination with certain dishes.

Sherry

Sherry is made in two basic styles, fino and oloroso, with a number of variations of each depending on ageing, blending and whether they are dry or sweet. As it is fortified after fermentation, all sherry is naturally dry. It is sweetened later for export or a house style.

Fino is the lightest, driest sherry, with a characteristic tang and

Ten top matches for sherry and port

Vintage port and Stilton
Aged tawny and warm chocolate soufflé pudding
Manzanilla and grilled prawns
Fino and spicy prawn wontons, deep-fried
Fino and fried fish salad
Fino and tempura
Amontillado and Wensleydale
Tawny port and walnut cake
Dry oloroso and mature Cheddar soufflé
Sweet sherry and trifle

yeasty flavour. This comes from flor, a local yeast which forms a blanket over the young wine and protects it from air while it matures. Its characteristics are most pronounced in manzanilla, which comes from the coastal town of Sanlúcar de Barrameda.

Fino and tapas is a classic in Jerez, as in much of Spain. The taste of the wine is an excellent match for the varied snacks of seafood, olives, salty local cheese, ham and little fried foods which make up a typical tapas selection. Fino is also good with oriental spring rolls or wonton dumplings, with tempura and other deep-fried vegetables or fish and with cold soups or avocado, peppers or tomatoes. Dry amontillado, which is an aged fino, is richer and nuttier in style and matches cheeses like Wensleydale, roasted nuts and warm salads based on nut oils, as well as some dried hams and sausages.

Dry, aged oloroso, which is relatively rare outside Spain, is very dark, rich and raisiny. It is a good accompaniment to meat soups, to olives and hard nutty cheeses such as mature Cheddar, Cheshire or Gouda. It is also an intriguing accompaniment to a cheese soufflé served with walnut salad or to roast teal.

Sweetened sherries match dark sticky cakes and puddings. Trifle is an obvious choice, but they also suit nut or biscuit cakes, rich creams and caramelised puddings including crème brûlée.

Port

There are three types of port: young, simple, fruity styles of white, ruby and tawny; aged tawny, which is aged in wood; and vintage, which is aged in the bottle. All are fortified early in fermentation and therefore retain sugar and are naturally sweet, though well-aged tawny is not intensely so, and certain white ports are made in a dry apéritif style.

Vintage port and Stilton is a great classic in the salt-sweet-fruit mould. In fact, port is a good choice for most strong, mature hard cheeses and so often suits the ubiquitous cheeseboard better than a light wine. Port and nuts are also a good ending to a meal, a combination which can be extended to tawny port and a nut cake, steamed walnut pudding, chocolate cake or soufflé-pudding, or a rich dark pastry of chocolate, nuts and spices. Tawny is also good to drink with delicate crisp biscuits or a plain cake.

8 PLANNING A MENU

Food and wine can nowadays provide a talking point and a well chosen menu often smooths a stiff or formal gathering. The choice of wine with a meal depends not only on the food, but on the whole occasion— the time, weather and company. Roast lamb served at a business dinner will have different requirements than at Sunday lunch. The style of wine should also suit the occasion—fine wines will be lost at a barbecue or multi-generation lunch.

A dinner party usually has three or four successive courses and different wines can be chosen to complement each dish. A simpler occasion may depend on only one wine, while the nightmare buffet usually calls for the safe option of one white and one red to accompany the range of foods and flavours as well as budgeting for a large number.

When planning a menu first decide on the number of wines to be served: a wine for each course or a more flexible choice for the whole meal. Fix a budget based on the number of guests and the occasion. You need to allow from a half to one bottle per person depending on the length of the meal.

Although dinner parties are less rigid now than a generation ago, the usual logical progression of courses provides structure for the choice of wine. Select the wine for the main course first, or if there is a difficult food like asparagus or smoked salmon then choose an appropriate wine and build the others around it.

One wine for the first course and one for the main is usually sufficient with perhaps a sweet or fortified 'bonne bouche' with the cheese or pudding. Too many different wines can detract from each other unless the meal is long or the purpose is to enjoy a number of wines in like-minded company. Serving wine as an apéritif not only helps the palate, but allows extra variety. On some occasions the apéritif wine can also be served with the first course.

For simpler meals, one wine or a choice of 'red or white' is the usual option. If serving one wine only, aim to match the main course with something which will not actually clash with the other foods. Relatively full, not too aromatic or oaky whites and light to medium-bodied reds are usually most flexible, especially New World Pinot Noir, southern French reds or Rioja.

Two wines give a bit more interest and flexibility. Try starting with a white to drink before the meal which will also match the first course. This allows for a full, rich or spicy red afterwards.

Buffet meals are often difficult because of the number of different flavours. Avoid wine with a lot of oak or tannin or anything too complex. Look for vibrant fruit or spicy flavours. Another option is to select a theme for the wine and food, say from a particular country or region. An Italian pasta is often a good centrepiece for a buffet which can be preceded by a colourful antipasta and accompanied by regional wines.

Champagne is a classic picnic choice and certainly adds glamour and romance to an al fresco occasion. Sparkling wines are a more reasonable option and can be very refreshing provided they can be kept cold. Otherwise simple, robust wines with plenty of flavour are best with outdoor food. It is not the time to savour delicacy or complexity so choose regional wines, those from assertive grape varieties, such as Sauvignon Blanc, or ripe, hot country fruit such as Australian Cabernet. Beaujolais or other young wines are also a good choice especially if served slightly cold, and are good with pâtés, cold meats and pies.

For barbecues choose oaky, well-flavoured wines to match the intense taste of charcoal-grilled food. Australian Chardonnay, Shiraz, Zinfandel as well as fruit-driven vin de pays, earthy Pinotage or a spicy Navarra all work well.

The traditional family Christmas is not the time for very fine wines. Food is copious in quantity and varied in flavour and for many people Christmas dinner comes at the end of a series of parties when neither palate nor concentration is at its best.

Champagne or sparkling wine is a good start as an apéritif. This will also go well with a first course of smoked salmon or shellfish.

Traditional turkey, especially if it has a fruity stuffing, suits either a full-bodied white wine such as a New World Chardonnay, or a medium-bodied red, a Grand Cru Beaujolais, Pinot Noir or Merlot which is not too oaky. Reserva Rioja is also successful, especially if the turkey is cooked with chestnuts.

Goose is much richer and needs a wine with tannin and acidity. A traditional combination is Riesling Spätlese or Vendange Tardive from Alsace. For a red wine, a Rhône or Haut Médoc is a classic choice; Chianti Riserva also works well or a really peppery Shiraz.

Dark plum pudding and mince pies are rich and spicy in flavour and also quite alcoholic. Fortified sweet wines are best: Muscats from the south of France or even Banyuls, port or a liqueur Muscat from Australia.

Serving order of wines

Just as food affects the taste of wine, so one wine affects the taste of another. When more than one wine is served at a meal, the order in which they are served is important. The general rule is the same as with food, that of balance between weight and complexity.

The usual pattern is to serve dry white wine before red; lighter wines before full-bodied heavier ones; young wines before old ones; dry before sweet and simple before complex.

The intention is that the weight and complexity builds up gradually. If you start with a very mature, complex or full-bodied wine, lesser wines which follow will be overshadowed and may seem thin, one-dimensional and certainly not at their best. For example, a full-bodied, barrel-fermented Californian Chardonnay could be followed by an Australian Shiraz, but a Chilean Merlot would seem rather light. Similarly, a vigourous young Rhône would appear simple, even clumsy after a ten-year-old claret.

The mixture of classic and New World wines is also an unhappy one, as the ripe fruit, high alcohol and intensity of the latter invariably overshadow the more subtle flavours of the traditional regions. If you want to serve a mixture, serve the New World last.

The requirements of food may occasionally upset the order for serving wine, when a first course or other dish needs a particular kind of wine. There are a number of examples which need special care.

Starting with a sweet wine

The classic combination of foie gras and Sauternes means that the meal opens with an intensely sweet, luscious wine. Such a first taste can make following dry wines, whites in particular, seem lean and unattractive, and bring up the tannins in red. although this does not seem to unduly bother the Bordelais.

Anything to follow Sauternes needs to be full-bodied and rich. If the food is suitable, another sweet wine, an Auslese Riesling for example, is fine though this does create a rather specialised menu. If you need to follow with a fine white, go for the full body of a Burgundy or Pinot Gris from Alsace and allow time to refresh the palate with bread or water in between.

Red wines too can suffer from lingering sweetness. Rich, spicy reds do best—Pinot Noir or Syrah or a Haut Médoc from a warm vintage, or good St Émilion or Pomerol. Again a pause to refresh the palate is a good idea.

Less sweet wines served at the start of a meal—Riesling Kabinett or Spätlese, off-dry Vouvray etc—also need full body, richness and fruit to follow, though their clean finish and high acidity is more helpful.

After oak

Full-bodied oaky white wines need a similarly weighty wine to follow. If you serve two white wines, start with the lighter wine with less oak. A following red wine should also be of equal or greater weight. After full, buttery Chardonnay, a red wine such as Beaujolais or AC Bordeaux will seem thin and simple. Richer reds from warm, ripe years and assertive grape varieties work best—Reserva Rioja, New World Cabernet and Shiraz or Rhône reds for example.

Old and new

Young wines have much simpler flavours which will show poorly after the complexity of a mature wine. It is better to build up to complexity. Often starting with a similar, younger wine is a good way to set the scene for a special, venerable bottle. Occasionally, vintages can be deceptive. It is important to remember that it is the maturity you taste, rather than the simple age. A younger wine from a 'forward' year may be better served after a more tannic, reserved vintage.

On the other hand a fragile old wine may well be overpowered by aggressive tannins in younger wines which have gone before; moderately mature wines are better, or else white wine or a gentler red such as St Émilion.

Matching Food and Wine

A red start

Certain first courses are best with red wine, notably pasta, some risottos and meat-based warm salads. At the main course you can stay with the same wine or move to a more full-bodied red, and perhaps serve a white wine apéritif for variety.

If the main dish needs a white wine, then choose a light-bodied red and a full white; the order is unconventional but often successful and amusing.

Matching the food to a special wine

Most of the time wines are chosen to match the food and menu, but occasionally a special bottle may be the star attraction and the menu is planned the other way round.

Fine wines usually show best against simple but refined food: fine claret with roast lamb, mature Burgundy with game, Pomerol with quail or guinea fowl, fine white Burgundy with roasted farm chicken, old Hermitage or Côte Rôtie with beef.

Highly flavoured sauces or other garnishes and spices are better avoided. Horseradish, mint sauce and fruity garnishes for game can be quite destructive, as can hot English mustard or garlic, or sage stuffings for poultry. The food does not have to be fine or special as long as the flavours are balanced.

Casseroles can work very well especially with mature Burgundy or north Italian reds.

Cold game is another, simple option which can be a good foil to a complex wine.

Fine white wine, mature Burgundy or Graves, a fine Alsace, Riesling or Grand Cru Chablis, for example, also shows best with relatively simple food—shellfish including lobster, certain cheeses or farm poultry cooked in butter are good options.

When serving a fine wine it is better to build up to it starting with something similar but younger or simpler. Too many fine, mature wines on the same occasion can be overpowering and detract from each other unless it is a dinner for enthusiasts especially devoted to wine.

INTRODUCTION TO THE RECIPES

The second part of this book is intended to help you put theory into practice.

Most of all, food and wine are to be enjoyed in good company, and meals at home for friends and family are some of the best opportunities to explore the real fun of matching food and wine.

The recipes in this section have been devised to be quite simple to prepare yet to give maximum flavour and excitement. They are also intended to show off the greatest possible range of wines and style across the globe.

Both wine and food are about flavour, feeding the senses as much as the rest of the body. Cooking at home, from day to day, at weekends or for entertaining friends, as well as meals in some of the excellent restaurants around the country, are ways to experience real food and the great range of ingredients and flavours now available.

This range of food needs a cautionary note. The current trend towards fusion or multicultural cuisine among professionals can lead to an excess of flavours and a lack of subtlety which will damage almost any wine it accompanies. Cooking, like winemaking, depends for its quality on balance which may include strong flavours, dramatic contrasts and unexpected effects but also needs restraint and finesse.

The following are useful points to bear in mind when cooking for wine:

Home-made stocks: meat and fish stocks, which can be bought from certain delicatessens, or made at home in large quantities to store in the freezer, are preferable to stock cubes.

Most *seasoning mixes and powders* are damaging to anything but the simplest wine as they accentuate tannin and oak flavours and are generally very salty. In the same way artificial flavours, essences etc. can upset the natural fruit in wine. Instead use herbs, carefully blended spices or other vegetable and natural flavours.

Low fat food is especially tricky with wine and substituting yoghurt for cream etc. can make foods less compatible, specifically by enhancing the acidity of the wine. With super lean food choose softer wines with low tannin and moderate acidity with plenty of ripe fruit.

Spices need careful use in food to accompany wine. Really hot foods are better avoided and also too many spices in one dish. Crudely used spices, especially white pepper, curry and chilli pepper, dull the palate and make it less appreciative of wine.

Simple foods can be very good foils to wine. Irish stew, shepherd's pie, good sausages, pasta with a home-made sauce or butter and cheese, roast chicken, even fish and chips can partner relatively fine wines.

Cooking with wine

The most important thing when using this magic ingredient is that it must be cooked. When wine is heated the acidity and alcohol become volatile, so it must be boiled or simmered to get rid of the harsh taste which results, leaving the flavour of wine and fruit. Rapid boiling for a minute or so, or long simmering are equally effective.

A wine for cooking should be fit to drink, in other words it should be fresh, not from a half full bottle left open for a week on the kitchen sideboard! Bottle ends can be kept for cooking if carefully stoppered, refrigerated and used quickly. Otherwise use a wine store system like vacuum storage or pour the remaining wine into a smaller bottle to exclude as much air as possible.

Ten top matches for favourite foods and wines

Fish and chips with Cava
Baked ham with mature Gran Reserva Rioja
Beef stew with mature Barolo
Shepherds pie with St Émillion
Sausages with Shiraz
Baked chicken with white Burgundy
Meatballs with Chilean Merlot
Spaghetti Bolognese with Rosso di Torgiano
Ratatouille with Rosé de Provence
Tuna fish bake with Australian barrel-fermented
   Chardonnay

Different types of wine have different effects. Medium sweet commercial whites lack acidity and are better avoided. Some red grape varieties give better colour than others, notably Merlot and Gamay. Sweet wines, and those which are notably aromatic such as Gewürztraminer, add extra flavours. Remember, too, that a boring wine will make a boring sauce, and though fine wines are certainly not required, a robust tasty red or crisp fruity white is most successful.

Fortified wines, especially the frequently misused sherry, should be used in extreme moderation.

9 APÉRITIF FOOD AND WINE

To begin a meal with a carefully chosen though simply prepared combination of canapés and wine is a novel and enjoyable idea. It is an especially easy way to start a summer party or barbecue, or a meal with large numbers. The trick is to choose a simple but striking combination.

Bruschetta with peppers and anchovies (serves 8)

2 red peppers
2 yellow peppers
5 tablespoons olive oil
12 slices ciabatta or similar bread
6 anchovy fillets

freshly ground black pepper
1–2 cloves garlic, peeled and cut in half
3 tablespoons grated Parmesan cheese

Method: Preheat oven to 200°C/400°F/gas mark 6.

Cut the peppers in half without removing the seeds or core and place skin side up in a roasting pan. Brush with olive oil and bake for 15 minutes until the skins are burnt and loose. Cool, then peel off the skin, remove the seeds and core and slice into strips about ½ inch/1 cm thick.

Bake the bread slices until crisp and tinged with gold. Chop the anchovies and mix with 3 tablespoons of olive oil and pepper. When the bread is ready, rub well with the cut garlic and spread with the anchovy oil. Top with the pepper slices and season with salt and pepper. Sprinkle with the Parmesan and remaining olive oil.

To serve: heat for 2–3 minutes in a warm oven and serve warm.

Wine: North Italian Tocai or Pinot Bianco.

Filo pastries (serves 8)

Filling

2 tablespoons vegetable oil

1 onion, finely chopped

2 cloves garlic, peeled and
finely chopped

8 oz/225 g turkey, minced

2 teaspoons curry powder

2 oz/50 g dried apricots, diced

2 oz/50 g almonds, skinned
and chopped

salt, freshly ground black
pepper

1 tablespoon tomato purée

4 fl oz/125 ml white wine

3 tablespoons parsley, finely
chopped

Pastries

4 large sheets filo pastry

2–3 oz/50–75 g butter, melted

Method: Preheat oven to 200°C/400°F/gas mark 6.

Heat the oil and cook the onion and garlic until soft. Add the minced turkey and cook until the meat and onions are well browned. Add the curry powder and stir for 1 minute, then lower the heat and add the apricots and almonds. Season to taste.

Add the tomato purée and wine, then cover and simmer gently for 20 minutes. Check that the mixture does not dry out and add a little water if needed. Stir in the parsley, check the seasoning and cool.

Make the pastries: lay a sheet of filo pastry on the work top, brush with butter and cut into 4 long strips. Place a spoonful of filling at one end of the strip and fold the corner over to make a triangle at the top of the pastry. Fold this triangle over on itself for the whole length of the pastry. Brush with more butter and place on a baking tray. Make up all the other pastries in the same way.

Bake the pastries for 15 minutes until golden and crisp.

To serve: serve warm or cool.

Wine: Chilean Sauvignon Blanc or light-bodied Pinotage.

Spicy chicken wings (serves 8)

2 lb/900 g chicken wings
Marinade
2 cloves garlic, peeled and
  crushed
4 tablespoons soy sauce
1 inch/2.5 cm piece root
  ginger, peeled and finely
  chopped

4 tablespoons sherry
2 tablespoons brown sugar
2 teaspoons cumin
2 teaspoons paprika
2 teaspoons sweet chilli sauce

Note: The chicken wings should be marinated for four hours or
overnight.

Method: Trim the chicken wings of excess skin. Make some
small cuts in the fleshy part to allow the marinade to penetrate.

Mix all the ingredients for the marinade and add the chicken
wings, turning and rubbing with the mixture to coat well. Leave
for 4 hours or overnight.

Preheat oven to 200°C/400°F/gas mark 6.

Spread out the wings in a roasting tin and bake for 30 minutes,
basting with the marinade occasionally.

To serve: arrange on a platter and serve warm.

Wine Grenache Rosé from Australia or another fruity rosé such
as one from Languedoc Roussillon.

Guacamole (serves 8)

2 ripe avocados
juice ½ lemon
1 tablespoon onion, peeled and
finely chopped
½ red pepper, finely chopped
½ green pepper, finely
chopped
2–3 cloves garlic, peeled and
finely chopped
½–1 green chilli, seeded and
finely chopped
2 tomatoes, peeled and
chopped
salt, freshly ground black
pepper
3 tablespoons coriander, finely
chopped
4–6 tablespoons virgin olive oil
1 stick of French bread strips
or 12 oz raw vegetables eg.
carrots, cucumber, cauli-
flower

Method: Peel the avocados and remove the stone from each. Mash the flesh well with a fork. Mix in the lemon juice to preserve the colour.

Mix the onion, peppers, garlic, chilli and tomato and mix into the avocado purée. Season to taste. Add the coriander and the olive oil to give a rich, soft consistency. Spoon into a shallow dish or bowl and cover well. Store in the fridge.

Cut the French bread into thin slices and bake until crisp or toast. Prepare the vegetables as appropriate. Chill until ready to serve.

To serve: serve at room temperature with the bread or crudités for dipping.

Wine: Cava or Chardonnay Vin de Pays d'Oc.

The opening of a meal should be light and stimulating in both food and wine. The ideal combination is interesting enough to catch attention and also set up the palate for richer tastes to follow.

Warm roasted vegetable salad (serves 8)

1 red pepper
1 green pepper
1 yellow pepper
4–6 tablespoons olive oil
2 large onions, peeled and diced
1 aubergine, diced
2 small courgettes, diced
8 cloves garlic, peeled
1 lb/450 g ripe tomatoes, peeled, seeded and chopped
salt, freshly ground black pepper
2 teaspoons cumin, ground
2–3 tablespoons fresh mint, chopped
zest and juice 1 lemon

Method: Preheat oven to 200°C/400°F/gas mark 6.

Grill or bake the peppers until the skin is black and charred, cool, peel off the skin, remove the seeds and cut into large dice.

Heat two tablespoons of olive oil in a shallow roasting dish, add the diced onions, aubergine, courgettes, whole garlic cloves and tomatoes. Season with salt and freshly ground pepper and roast for 15 minutes. Stir occasionally. Add the cumin and peppers and roast for 5–10 minutes more until the vegetables are tender and tinged with colour.

Stir in the remaining olive oil, mint, lemon zest and juice and season to taste.

To serve: serve warm or at room temperature with crusty bread.

Wine: Jurançon Sec, Gewürztraminer or young Tokay Pinot Gris.

Onion tarts (serves 8)

12 oz/350 g puff pastry
flour to roll out
Filling
1½ lb/700 g onions, peeled
   and very thinly sliced
2 tablespoons olive oil
1 oz/25 g butter

4 eggs
3 eggs yolks
½ pint/275 ml cream
4 fl oz/110 ml milk
3 oz/75 g gruyère cheese
salt, freshly ground black
   pepper

Method: Preheat oven to 220°C/425°F/gas mark 7. Take 8 x 3 inch/10 cm tartlet tins. Roll out the pastry thinly and line the tins. Prick the pastry very well and chill for at least 30 minutes. Line each pastry case with greaseproof paper and fill with beans or rice. Bake blind for 8–10 minutes until golden and set, thenremove the paper and beans and cool.

Make the filling: cook the onions gently in the oil and butter for about 30 minutes until soft and just turning golden. Whisk the eggs, yolks, cream and milk in a bowl, add the onions, half the cheese and seasoning to taste.

Sprinkle the bottom of each tartlet with the remaining cheese and carefully pour in the filling, making sure to distribute the onions evenly. Lower the oven to 190°C/375°F/gas mark 5 and bake for about 20 minutes until the filling is set and golden on top. Leave to stand for 5 minutes.

To serve: remove from the tins and serve immediately.

Wine: Alsace Riesling, or Rhine Riesling Kabinett, from Rheingau or Nahe preferably. For a simpler occasion, try Silvaner.

Smoked salmon and smoked haddock salad with dill (serves 8)

1 head chicory
1 butterhead lettuce
1 bunch watercress
8 oz/225 g smoked salmon
1 oz/25 g walnuts, finely chopped

Dressing
2 tablespoons lemon juice
½ teaspoon Dijon mustard
salt, freshly ground black pepper
2 tablespoons light olive oil
6 tablespoons walnut oil
zest of ½ lemon, finely grated
2 tablespoons chives, chopped
12 oz/350 g smoked haddock
5 fl oz/150 ml cream
3 tablespoons dill, finely chopped

Method: Clean and dry the salad leaves, shred the chicory, tear the butterhead into pieces and remove the watercress leaves from stalks. Place in a large salad bowl.

Trim the smoked salmon and cut into fine strips. Close to serving time mix with the salad leaves and walnuts.

Make the dressing: mix the lemon juice, mustard, salt and pepper. Whisk in the oils, then add the lemon zest and chives.

Remove any bones or skin from the haddock. Slice into fine medallions about ¼ inch /½ cm thick. Bring the cream and dill to the boil, add the pepper and carefully add the medallions of haddock. Poach gently for 2–3 minutes.

To serve: toss the salad leaves and smoked salmon with the dressing and place a portion in the centre of each plate. Place 3 medallions of haddock around the edge of each plate with a little of the dill cream spooned over.

Wine: barrel-fermented New Zealand Chardonnay or cool-climate Chardonnay from South Africa or Casablanca in Chile.

Mushroom risotto (serves 4)

4 oz/110 g oyster mushrooms
1 tablespoon olive oil
1½ pints/855 ml well-fla-
  voured chicken stock
2 oz/50 g butter
1 small onion, peeled and
  finely chopped
8 oz/225 g wild mushrooms—
  cèpes, trompettes, bolets etc

12 oz/350 g risotto rice
4 fl oz/110 ml white wine
salt, freshly ground black
  pepper
2 oz/50 g Parmesan cheese,
  grated
1 oz/25 g Parmesan cheese,
  shaved into large flakes

Method: Quickly fry the oyster mushrooms in a little hot oil, drain on kitchen paper and reserve.

Heat the chicken stock in a saucepan until boiling, then turn down the heat but keep very hot.

Heat the butter in a large pan, add the onion and cook for 2–3 minutes until soft but not coloured. Add the wild mushrooms and cook for 1–2 minutes then stir in the rice and cook, stirring, constantly until well coated with butter and thoroughly heated. Add the wine and cook, stirring, until evaporated. Gradually add the hot stock, a ladle at a time, allowing the rice to absorb all the stock before adding more. Stir very frequently and season to taste with salt and pepper. The risotto takes 20 minutes to cook.

When the risotto is cooked but still moist and creamy in consistency, add the grated Parmesan.

To serve: serve immediately in individual portions, garnished with the oyster mushrooms and flakes of Parmesan.

Wine: Chablis or dry Vouvray, or for a more unusual match try mature Côte de Beaune, or 5–10 year-old Chinon, both of which are sensational with this dish.

Goats' cheese salad (serves 8)

1 head curly endive
1 head oakleaf lettuce
4 pears
1 oz/25 g butter
2 oz/50 g sugar
juice ° lemon
12 oz/350 g cylindrical goats' cheese
freshly ground black pepper
2–3 tablespoons creamy honey

2 oz/50 g dry breadcrumbs
Dressing
2 tablespoons red wine vinegar
1 teaspoon Dijon mustard
1 teaspoon wholegrain mustard
salt, freshly ground black pepper
4 tablespoons light olive oil
4 tablespoons hazelnut oil

Method: Wash and dry the salad leaves and place in a large bowl. Peel and core the pears and cut each into 8 slices. Heat the butter, sugar and lemon juice in a wide pan, add the pear slices and cook for 5–10 minutes until soft and golden. Remove and cool.

Remove the rind from the cheese and slice into 8 discs, about ° inch/1 cm thick. Season with pepper and spread the honey over the top of each disc. Coat the top with breadcrumbs. Place on a baking sheet and chill until serving—do not leave for longer than 1 hour.

Make the dressing: mix the vinegar, mustards and seasoning, then whisk in the oils.

Place the cheese under a hot grill and cook until golden—2–3 minutes.

To serve: toss the salad leaves with half the dressing and divide between 8 plates. Arrange 4 slices of caramelised pear around the edge and top each salad with the grilled cheese. Sprinkle the remaining dressing around the plate attractively and serve immediately.

Wine: Vouvray Mousseux or demi-sec, Sancerre or New Zealand Sauvignon Blanc.

moked haddock and cheese soufflé (serves 8)

oz/225 g smoked haddock
lb/450 g fresh spinach
tablespoon oil
oz/25 g butter
lt, freshly ground black
  pepper
tablespoons cream
ice ½ lemon
oufflé
utter for the dishes
oz/50 g butter

2 oz/50 g flour
½ pint/275 ml milk
4 oz/110 g mature cheddar
  cheese, grated
1 teaspoon Dijon mustard
salt, freshly ground black
  pepper
6 eggs, separated
salt, freshly ground black
  pepper

Method: Preheat oven to 200°C/400°F/gas mark 6.

Cut the haddock into dice, removing any skin or bone. Clean
ne spinach and fry it for about 30 seconds or until it has
ilted—in the oil. Drain. Heat the butter, add the haddock and
ook for 1–2 minutes, then add the spinach and seasoning and
:ir in the cream. Add lemon juice to taste.

Butter 8 ramekin or small soufflé dishes. Spoon a little of the
addock and spinach mixture into each.

Make the soufflé: melt the butter and stir in the flour, cook
ently for 3 minutes then gradually add the milk, stirring all the
me. Stir in the cheese, remove from the heat and add the
nustard and seasoning. Beat in the egg yolks. Whisk the egg
hites until stiff and stir about one-third through the mixture.
old in the remaining whites and spoon into the soufflé dishes.

Stand the soufflé dishes in a shallow pan in about ½ inch/1 cm
ater then transfer to the oven and bake for 15 minutes until
uffed and golden but still slightly soft in the centre. Serve at
nce.

Wine: Montagny Blanc, Rully or Mâcon Villages.

Scallops with lemon grass butter (serves 8)

24 fresh scallops
1 tablespoon olive oil for
  frying
Lemon grass butter
2 strands lemon grass, chopped
  finely into dishes
2 tablespoons white wine
  vinegar
6 tablespoons white wine
3–4 tablespoons cream

10 oz/275 g butter
salt, freshly ground black
  pepper
juice ½ to 1 lemon
2 tablespoons fresh coriander,
  chopped
Bok choy
2–3 heads bok choy greens,
  cleaned
salt

Method: Cut the scallops into 3–4 thin discs through the thickness.

Make the sauce: combine the lemon grass with the vinegar and wine. Boil until reduced to a few spoons of liquid. Add the cream and boil for a minute or two. Gradually whisk in the butter without allowing the sauce to boil. Season with salt and pepper and add lemon juice to taste. Pass through a sieve. Stir in the coriander. Keep warm over hot, not boiling, water.

Steam the bok choy: cut the bok choy into 3 or 4 wedges and place in a steamer. Cook over boiling salted water for about 4 minutes, until just tender.

Cook the scallops: heat a non-stick pan and cook the scallop pieces quickly, for about 30 seconds each side.

To serve: place a piece of bok choy on each plate, pour around the sauce and arrange the slices of scallop on top. Serve immediately.

Wine: Riesling Kabinett from the Mosel or Rheingau, or New Zealand Riesling.

Smoked eel salad (serves 8)

12 oz/350 g smoked eel,
  skinned

Salad

oakleaf lettuce, washed and
  dried

small carrots, peeled, cut
  into julienne strips and
  blanched

sticks celery, cut in julienne
  strips

oz/50 g fine green beans,
  blanched and cut into ½
  inch/1 cm pieces

1 lemon

Dressing

1 tablespoon lemon juice

salt, freshly ground black
  pepper

1 tablespoon olive oil

3 tablespoons walnut oil

Dill cream

4 fl oz/110 ml yoghurt

2 fl oz/55 ml cream

salt, freshly ground black
  pepper

2 tablespoons dill, finely
  chopped

Method: Cut the eel into strips about 2 inches/5 cm long and ¼ inch/½ cm wide. Cover with cling film until ready to serve.

Prepare the salad: remove the centre stalks from the lettuce leaves and tear into pieces. Combine with the vegetables. Grate the zest from the lemon and add to the vegetables. Remove the eel segments from the membrane and dice the flesh. Add to the vegetables.

Make the dressing: combine all the ingredients and mix well. Add to the vegetables and toss.

Make the dill cream: mix the yoghurt and cream and stir in the dill. Season to taste.

To serve: arrange some eel on each plate, add a small pile of salad and garnish with dill cream.

Wine: Riesling Kabinett.

Mussel feuilletés (serves 8)

Carrot purée
1½ lb/700 g carrots
1 oz/25 g butter
salt, freshly ground black
  pepper
1 tablespoon sugar
2–3 tablespoons crème fraîche
Pastries
8 oz/225 g puff pastry
flour to roll out
1 egg, beaten
Mussels
1 oz/25 g butter
2 shallots
1 clove garlic peeled

3 sprigs parsley
3 fl oz/75 ml white wine
3 thin slices root ginger, peeled
3 lb/1350 g fresh mussels,
  cleaned
Sauce
½ teaspoon saffron strands
juice from mussels
½ pint/425 ml cream
juice 1 lime
2 tablespoons preserved ginger,
  chopped
2 tablespoons fresh coriander,
  chopped

Method: Preheat oven to 200°C/400°F/gas mark 6.

Make the carrot purée: peel and slice the carrots finely. Place in a saucepan with the butter, seasoning and 6 tablespoons of water. Cover tightly and cook for about 8 minutes until tender, and most of the liquid has been absorbed. Blend to a purée then add the crème fraîche and check seasoning.

Make the feuilletés: roll out the puff pastry and cut into 8 rectangles or make 8 shapes using a small scallop shell. Brush with beaten egg and mark decoratively with the point of a knife, following the marking of the shell if using, or make a criss-cross pattern. Place on a baking tray and chill.

Cook the mussels: melt the butter in a large pan, add the shallots, garlic and parsley, then pour in the wine. Add the ginger and the cleaned mussels, cover and cook for about 3 minutes until the mussels open. Drain, reserving the juices, and cool the mussels before removing from shells.

Bake the pastries for 10 minutes until deep golden and well puffed. Cool, then carefully split in half.

Make the sauce: Pass the mussel juice through a sieve. Add a little of the warm juice to the saffron to release the colour. Boil the remaining mussel juice until well concentrated, then add the cream and saffron juice and simmer for 5 minutes. Add the lime juice and season to taste. Stir in the ginger, coriander and shelled mussels.

Spread the bottom half of each pastry with some of the carrot purée and re-heat gently in the oven with the pastry lids.

To serve: arrange a pastry base on each plate, spoon the mussels and sauce on top and around and cover with the lid. Garnish with coriander. Serve immediately.

Wine: Savennières or Australian Marsanne.

Bean soup with mushrooms (serves 8)

8 oz/225 g dried cannellini
  beans, soaked overnight
8 oz/225 g wild or cultivated
  mushrooms, sliced
3 cloves garlic, peeled and
  crushed
4 tablespoons olive oil
2 onions, finely chopped

1 bunch parsley, thyme and
  marjoram, finely chopped
1 sprig rosemary
salt, freshly ground black
  pepper
1½–2 pints/845–1130 ml
  chicken stock
6 tablespoons cream
1 oz/25 g butter

Method: Drain the beans, place in a saucepan and cover with about 1½ pints/¾ litres fresh water. Bring to the boil, cook rapidly for 10 minutes, then simmer for 1 hour.

Sauté the mushrooms in 1 tablespoon of oil with the garlic.

Heat 3 tablespoons olive oil and cook the onions until soft. Drain the beans and add to the onions with the herbs and seasoning, half the sautéed mushrooms, and the chicken stock. Cook for 20 minutes.

When the soup is cooked blend to a purée or work through a ricer. Re-heat the soup and add the cream. Season to taste. Add the butter and whisk, shaking the pan rapidly to incorporate.

To serve: place some reserved mushrooms in each bowl and ladle the soup into bowls. Serve immediately.

Wine: Vernaccia di San Gimignano.

Marinated fish with herbs (serves 8)

1¼ lb/560 g brill, skinned
juice 2 limes
1 bulb fennel
1 tablespoon white wine
    vinegar
2 teaspoons coriander seeds
salt, freshly ground black
    pepper
Dressing
2 tablespoons fresh coriander,
    finely chopped

2 tablespoons fennel, finely
    chopped
2 tablespoons chervil, finely
    chopped
2 limes
5 fl oz/150 ml olive oil
salt, freshly ground black
    pepper
2 tomatoes, peeled, seeded and
    chopped

Method: Cut the brill into very fine slices, like smoked salmon. Place in a porcelain dish and pour over the lime juice. Leave to marinate in the fridge for at least 45 minutes.

Trim the fennel bulb and cut into four pieces. Cook in boiling water with the vinegar, coriander and seasoning until tender, about 5 minutes. Drain and cool then slice thinly. Reserve.

Make the dressing: combine the herbs with the lime juice and olive oil and season well.

To serve: arrange some fennel on each plate, drain the slices of fish and arrange on top, spoon over the dressing and scatter with tomato dice.

Wine: Sancerre or Pouilly Fumé.

Ravioli with prawns and coriander (serves 8)

Ravioli

14 oz/400 g pasta flour or strong flour

1 teaspoon salt

3 eggs

3 egg yolks

2 tablespoons olive oil

Filling

8 oz/225 g brill or sole, skinned

½ oz/10 g butter

2 tablespoons white wine or fish stock

4oz/11g fresh prawns, peeled

½ inch/1 cm piece root ginger, peeled and finely chopped

1 teaspoon green chilli, seeded and chopped

3 tablespoons fresh coriander, chopped, stalks reserved

1 clove garlic, peeled and finely chopped

3 oz/75 g ricotta cheese

salt, freshly ground black pepper

Sauce

2 tablespoons white wine vinegar

6 tablespoons white wine

stalks from coriander

zest and juice 1 lime

3 tablespoons cream

10 oz/275 g butter

salt, freshly ground black pepper

Note: Pasta dough needs to be left for 2 hours or overnight before rolling.

Method: Make the pasta dough: place the flour and salt in a food processor or mixer. Add the eggs, yolks and olive oil and work until almost a dough, then remove from the machine and knead by hand for 1–2 minutes. Wrap the dough in cling film and leave in a cool place for at least 2 hours or overnight.

Make the filling: cook the fish quickly in a saucepan in the butter and wine or stock. Cool. Chop the prawns and place in a bowl with the root ginger, coriander, chilli and garlic. Flake the cooled fish and add to the other ingredients with the ricotta. Mix and season.

Fill the ravioli: cut the pasta dough into four. Roll out each piece in a machine or by hand, fold in 3, then roll out again.

Repeat until the dough is smooth, then roll out very thinly. Cut each thin piece of pasta into 36 discs about 2½ inches/7 cm in diameter. Discard the remaining dough (or roll and cut for noodles). Brush the edges of half the discs with water, place a teaspoon of filling in the centre of each and cover with another disc. Seal the edges well making sure to exclude all air from the filling. Place on a floured tray, cover lightly with a cloth or cling film and chill until ready to cook.

Make the sauce: boil the vinegar, wine, coriander stalks and lime zest until reduced to a few tablespoons of liquid. Add the cream and boil for 1–2 minutes. Gradually whisk in the butter without allowing the sauce to boil. Finally add the seasoning and lime juice to taste. Pass through a sieve and keep warm over hot but not boiling water.

Bring a large pot of water to the boil, season with salt and cook the ravioli for about 3 minutes. Drain.

To serve: Arrange 4 ravioli on each plate, spoon over the sauce and garnish with coriander leaves. Serve immediately.

Wine: New Zealand Riesling.

Melon and ham (serves 8)

2 ripe well flavoured melons, e.g. Galia or Charentais
4–6 tablespoons dry Muscat wine

12 oz/350 g Parma ham or similar high quality air-dried ham, very thinly sliced
freshly ground black pepper

Method: Cut the melon in half and remove the seeds. Cut into quarters and peel. Slice carefully into thin strips following the shape of the fruit. Place on a dish and pour the wine over

To serve: Arrange the ham on a platter or individual plates. Garnish with the melon, making a fan shape out of the slices for each portion. Season lightly with black pepper. Serve at once.

Wine: Dry Muscat.

Tabouleh with prawns (serves 8)

Prawns
12 oz/350 g tiger prawns
2 teaspoons coriander, ground
1 teaspoon paprika
1 clove garlic, crushed
2 tablespoons olive oil
Tabouleh
8 oz/225 g bulgur wheat
6 spring onions, finely
    chopped
2–3 cloves garlic, peeled and
    finely chopped
2 tablespoons coriander, finely
    chopped
7 tablespoons parsley, finely
    chopped

juice 1–2 lemons
6 tablespoons olive oil
salt, freshly ground black
    pepper
4 tomatoes, peeled, seeded and
    chopped
Dressing
6–8 tablespoons olive oil
1 red pepper, finely chopped
½ red chilli, seeds removed
    and finely chopped
2 teaspoons tomato purée
salt, freshly ground black
    pepper
½ teaspoon sugar
2 tablespoons balsamic vinegar

Method: Mix the prawns with the spices, garlic and olive oil
and leave for about 30 minutes.

Place the bulgur in a large bowl, pour the boiling water over to
cover the wheat by 1 inch/2 cm and leave to soak for about 15
minutes until the water is absorbed.

Stir the spring onions, garlic and herbs into the bulgur with the
lemon juice, 6 tablespoons of olive oil and seasoning. Then add
the tomatoes and stir in.

Carefully oil eight ramekins with the remaining tablespoon of
oil, spoon in the tabouleh and press down well. Cover the ramekins with foil. When ready to serve, heat gently in a warm oven
for 5–10 minutes.

Make the dressing: warm the olive oil, pepper, chilli, tomato
purée and seasoning without allowing to boil. Add the vinegar
and reserve.Quickly stir-fry the prawns. Cool.

To serve: Turn the bulgur on to individual plates, garnish with the prawns and spoon over the dressing. Decorate with coriander leaves and lemon slices.

Wine: New Zealand or Chilean Sauvignon Blanc; or Sauvignon-influenced vin de pays from the Loire.

Gazpacho (serves 8)

Soup

½ lb/700 g ripe tomatoes, peeled and chopped

3 sticks celery, chopped

½ cucumber, chopped

1 green pepper, chopped

1 red pepper, chopped

1 red onion, chopped

2 tablespoons parsley, chopped

1 tablespoon chives, chopped

3–4 cloves garlic, peeled and crushed

2 slices loose-textured country bread

6 tablespoons olive oil

salt, freshly ground black pepper

2–3 teaspoons sugar

2–3 tablespoon wine vinegar

½–1 pint/¼-½ litre water

tomato purée if necessary

Garnish

about 6 tablespoons good quality virgin olive oil

Note: The vegetables for the soup need to marinate overnight.

Method: Place all the ingredients for the soup, except the water, in a bowl, mixing well to coat everything with olive oil. Cover and marinate overnight.

Next day, blend the soup to a purée, adding enough water to give a rich consistency and adding tomato purée for colour if necessary. Check the seasoning and stir in the vinegar to taste.

Chill well.

To serve: Serve garnished with a little olive oil dribbled on each portion.

Wine: Fino sherry, chilled.

Risotto cakes with courgette and tomato (serves 8)

Risotto
1½ pints/845 ml vegetable or
  chicken stock
4 tablespoons olive oil
2 oz/50 g butter
1 small onion, finely chopped
12 oz/350 g risotto rice
5 fl oz/150 ml white wine
salt, freshly ground black
  pepper
3 tablespoons fresh basil,
  chopped
2 tablespoons chives, chopped
2 tablespoons parsley, chopped
1 teaspoon rosemary, chopped
3 oz Parmesan cheese, grated

Courgettes
4–6 small courgettes
oil for grill
1 clove garlic, peeled and
  crushed
3 tablespoons white wine
2 tablespoons olive oil
1 tablespoon basil, chopped
Tomato compote
2 tablespoons olive oil
1 tablespoon oil from sundried
  tomatoes
1 lb/450 g plum tomatoes,
  peeled and chopped into 8
  pieces each
2 cloves garlic, finely peeled and
  chopped
1 bunch basil, chopped
2 sundried tomatoes, chopped
1 oz/25 g black olives, stoned

Method: Make the risotto: bring the stock to the boil and keep very hot. Heat the oil and butter and cook the onion until transparent. Add the rice and cook until well coated in butter, hot and glistening. Add the wine, boil to evaporate, then add a ladleful of stock. Boil the rice, adding more stock as it is absorbed, stirring frequently and seasoning with salt and pepper. Towards the end of cooking add the herbs. The risotto takes 20 minutes to cook. Stir in the Parmesan, check the seasoning and turn the cooked risotto into a bowl to cool.

Prepare the courgettes: trim the courgettes and slice longways into strips about 1/8th inch/2 mm thick. Heat the grill and brush with oil. Season the courgette strips and cook for about 2 minutes on each side. Transfer to a dish and pour over the garlic, wine, olive oil and basil.

Make the tomato compote: heat the oils, add the tomatoes, garlic and basil and season to taste. Add the sundried tomatoes and cook for 5–10 minutes until the consistency is jam-like.

Add the olives and remove the basil stalks.

Make the risotto cakes: take tablespoons of the risotto and shape into little flat cakes; this quantity makes about 16. Heat the remaining oil and cook the cakes for 2 minutes on each side, turning carefully, until golden and hot.

To serve: reheat the courgettes and compote if necessary. Place two risotto cakes on each plate, place some courgette strips around them and top with tomato compote. Garnish with herbs and flaked Parmesan. Serve immediately.

Wine: good quality Anjou Blanc or a light, fruity red, such as Saumur-Champigny, served cool, or Italian Merlot.

If you serve a salad with a main dish use good quality wine or sherry vinegar, or balsamic vinegar if appropriate, and make the dressing with one part vinegar to four parts olive oil. If you are serving an old, fine wine, substitute wine for the vinegar.

Mushroom-stuffed quail (serves 8)

Stuffing

1 oz/25 g dried cèpes, soaked in hot water for 15 minutes, drained and chopped

2 tablespoons olive oil

2 shallots, peeled and finely chopped

2 teaspoons fresh sage, chopped

6 oz/175 g wild or cultivated mushrooms, finely chopped

salt, freshly ground black pepper

4 oz/110 g chicken breast

1 egg white

2–4 tablespoons cream

8 quail, boned

salt, freshly ground black pepper

2 tablespoons vegetable oil

Sauce

4 fl oz/110 ml red wine

1 sprig thyme

1 clove garlic, lightly crushed

12 fl oz/330 ml chicken or quail stock

salt, freshly ground black pepper

Method: Preheat oven to 190°C/375°F/gas mark 5.

Soak the cèpes in hot water for 15 minutes, then drain and chop them.

Make the stuffing: heat the oil and cook the shallots for 2–3 minutes. Add the sage and mushrooms, dried and fresh, and cook for about 5 minutes more. Season with salt and pepper and cool.

Place the chicken breast in a food processor and mince very finely. Work in the egg white and turn into a bowl. Stir in the cooled mushrooms and the cream. Season.

Lay the quail out flat and season with salt and pepper.

Place about 1 heaped teaspoon of stuffing in the body of each quail and wrap the sides and legs around to reform the shape as near as possible. Tie securely then chill until ready to cook.

Heat the oil in a large pan and brown the quail on all sides, turning carefully. Transfer to a tin and roast for 15 minutes.

Make the sauce: reduce the wine, thyme and garlic to a few spoonfuls of liquid, add the stock and reduce again until concentrated and dark. Season and pass through a sieve. Reheat before serving.

Rest the quail for 5 minutes out of the oven.

To serve: slice each quail and place in an overlapping row in the centre of the plate. Pour the sauce around.

To accompany: celeriac purée and some simply cooked spinach.

Wine: Pomerol (7–8 years old), mature Burgundy or Chianti Rufina Riserva; old Pesquera is also excellent.

Salmon with leeks (serves 8)

2½ lb/1k g filleted salmon, skinned

1 lb/450 g young leeks, cleaned

1 tablespoon white wine

Sauce

2 tablespoons white wine vinegar

4 tablespoons white wine

3 tablespoons cream

10 oz/275 g butter

salt, freshly ground black pepper

1 tablespoon wholegrain mustard

1 tablespoon vegetable oil for frying

Method: Cut the salmon into 8 portions. Slice the leeks longways into thin strips. Heat a little water and white wine in a saucepan, add the leeks and cook rapidly for about 5 minutes until tender. Drain, reserving the liquid.

Make the sauce: boil the vinegar, wine and liquid from the leeks until reduced to a few spoonfuls. Add the cream and simmer for 1–2 minutes or so. Gradually whisk in the butter, without allowing the sauce to boil. Season with salt and pepper and pass through a sieve. Stir in the mustard. Keep warm over hot, not boiling, water.

Heat the oil in a wide frying pan. Season the salmon slices with salt and pepper and cook for about 4 minutes each side until tender and pale golden. Rest the fish for 5 minutes after cooking.

To serve: twist the leeks around a carving fork then slide carefully on to the plate. Pour the sauce over the leeks and around the plate then place the salmon on top.

To accompany: plain boiled potatoes scattered with chopped parsley and chives.

Wine: Pouilly Fumé or dry white Graves.

Lamb and aubergine stew (serves 8)

3 lb/1.25 kg shoulder lamb, boned

salt, freshly ground black pepper

3 tablespoons olive oil

2 onions, peeled and finely chopped

2 aubergines, diced

3 cloves garlic, peeled and finely chopped

2 teaspoons cumin, ground

1 teaspoon cinnamon, ground

4 fl oz/110 ml red wine

3 tablespoons fresh oregano

1 can tomatoes

½ pint/275 ml stock, lamb or chicken

Method: Cut the lamb into cubes, removing excess fat. Season well with salt and pepper.

Heat 1 tablespoon of oil in a frying pan and brown the lamb cubes in batches until well coloured on all sides. Reserve the lamb on a plate. Pour 4 tablespoons of water into the frying pan and boil up, stirring and scraping to remove sediment, then pour off and reserve for later.

In a heavy casserole, heat the remaining oil and cook the onion for 5 minutes. Add the aubergine and cook for another 8 minutes until the onion and aubergine are softening and just golden. Add more oil if needed.

Return the meat to the pan. Add the garlic and spices. Stir and cook until everything is very hot. Pour in the wine and boil up for 1–2 minutes, stirring all the time. Add the tomatoes, oregano and stock, bring to the boil and turn down to simmer very gently for 1½ hours until the lamb is tender. Remove the lid for the last 20 minutes to reduce the sauce. Check the seasoning before serving.

To serve: serve straight from the casserole

To accompany: pilaff rice with raisins and pinenuts or some steamed couscous

Wine: red Coteaux du Languedoc, especially Faugères or Minervois.

Roast pork with fennel (serves 8)

Herb mixture
6 cloves garlic, peeled
1 tablespoon fennel seeds
4 tablespoons fennel herb, chopped
2 tablespoons chives, chopped
2 tablespoons parsley, chopped
salt, freshly ground black pepper

4 tablespoons olive oil
4 lb/2 k g boned loin pork, rind and some of the fat removed
coarse salt
½ pint/275 ml white wine
2–3 tablespoons fennel herb, chopped

Method: Preheat oven to 190°C/375°F/gas mark 5.

Place the garlic and fennel seeds in a mortar and crush; add the chopped herbs, seasoning and olive oil and mix well.

Lay the pork out flat, meat side upwards. Make some deep incisions into the meat with the point of a knife, about every inch. Rub the meat thoroughly with the herb and garlic mixture, making sure it reaches into the incisions. Roll and tie the meat tomake a neat shape. Sprinkle the outside with any remaining herb mixture and season well with coarse salt.

Heat a roasting tin and brown the meat on all sides. Roast for 1 hour, then cover with foil and leave to rest at room temperature for 15 minutes.

Add the wine to the juices in the roasting pan and boil rapidly, stirring and scraping the pan. Pass through a sieve and add the fennel. Check seasoning.

To serve: carve the pork in thick slices and serve with gravy.

To accompany: potato purée and French beans.

Wine: oak-aged Barbera d'Alba, Rosso di Montalcino or Rosso Conero.

Squid with sun-dried tomatoes and pasta (serves 8)

3 squid, cleaned
salt, freshly ground black
   pepper
3 tablespoons olive oil
3–4 cloves garlic, peeled
1 teaspoon fennel seeds,
   crushed
3 pieces star anise, crushed
   very lightly

4 fl oz/110 ml white wine
6 sundried tomatoes, chopped
2 lb/1 k g ripe plum tomatoes,
   peeled and chopped
1 lb/450 g fresh or dried
   tagliatelle
3 tablespoons shredded basil
2 oz/50 g black olives, stoned

Method: Slice the squid body into thin rings and the tentacles into strips. Season with salt and pepper.

Heat the olive oil in a heavy sauté pan and cook the squid for 5 minutes over a moderate heat. Add the garlic, fennel seeds and star anise and cook for 1 minute. Pour in the wine and boil up, then reduce the heat, add the sundried and fresh tomatoes and simmer, covered for 30 minutes. Check from time to time and keep the heat low.

Bring a large pan of water to the boil, add salt and cook the pasta, allowing 3–4 minutes for fresh pasta, and following the instructions for dried pasta. Drain and toss with olive oil and seasoning.

Add the basil and olives to the squid and toss with the pasta. Season to taste and serve immediately.

To accompany: a green salad with balsamic vinegar dressing and flakes of whole Parmesan, and some crusty bread

Wine: Australian Semillon or lightly-oaked Chardonnay.

Scallops with pasta and pancetta (serves 8)

12–16 scallops, cleaned
2 tablespoons olive oil
4 oz/110 g pancetta, diced
2 fl oz/55 ml white wine
½ pint/275 ml cream

salt, freshly ground black
  pepper
2 tablespoons chives, chopped
1 lb/450 g angel hair pasta,
  fresh or dried

Method: Cut the scallops through the thickness in 2 or 3 discs, depending on size.

Heat the oil, add the pancetta and cook for about 3 minutes until just golden. Add the wine and simmer for 1 minute, then add the cream and simmer to reduce slightly. Season with salt and pepper to taste and add the chives.

Bring a large pan of water to the boil and cook the pasta for 2–3 minutes for fresh or as directed for dried. Drain.

Heat a non-stick pan and cook the scallops for 30 seconds on each side. Toss the pasta with the cream and pancetta mixture until very hot.

To serve: arrange on individual plates and top with slices of scallop.

To accompany: a green salad and crusty bread

Wine: Chablis or Pinot Blanc.

Magret of duck with sherry vinegar (serves 8)

Sauce
1 tablespoon vegetable oil
12 shallots, peeled
6 cloves garlic, unpeeled
½ oz/10 g butter
1 tablespoon sugar
2 fl oz/55 ml sherry vinegar
2 teaspoons tomato purée
4 fl oz/110 ml white wine
½ pint/275 ml chicken or
    duck stock

2 sprigs rosemary
salt, freshly ground black
    pepper

8 duck breasts, boned
salt, freshly ground black
    pepper
4 tablespoons sherry vinegar
2–3 tablespoons honey

3 tablespoons sultanas, soaked
    in dry sherry

Method: Preheat oven to 200°C/400°F/gas mark 6.

Make the sauce: heat the oil in a large, wide pan. Add the shallots and garlic cloves and cook for 2–3 minutes stirring. Add the butter and sugar and cook and stir until it caramelises. Pour in the vinegar and boil rapidly for 1 minute. Add the tomato purée, wine, stock and rosemary and season. Simmer for 20 minutes. Remove the rosemary.

Trim the duck breasts and cut the fat in a few places to prevent curling up during cooking. Season well. Cook the duck, skin side down, in a frying pan over a moderate heat for about 5 minutes until crisp and golden. Turn and cook for 1 minute on the other side. Pour over the vinegar, boil up, then transfer the duck to a baking tray, fat side up. Brush with honey and roast for 4 minutes. Remove from the oven and baking sheet and rest for 5 minutes. Add the soaked sultanas with the sherry to the sauce and bring back to just below boiling.

To serve: carve each duck breast carefully and arrange in a fan shape on each plate with the pink of the meat showing.

To accompany: spinach tossed in olive oil and, on the side, a purée of parsnips and Bramley apples.

Wine: lighter style Amarone, or Carmignano Riserva.

Provençale vegetable gâteau (serves 8)

2 red peppers
2 yellow peppers
Sauce
2 tablespoons olive oil
1 onion, peeled and finely
  chopped
2 cloves garlic, finely chopped
1 teaspoon red chilli seeded
  and chopped
2 cans tomatoes
1 teaspoon sugar

salt, freshly ground black
  pepper
2 tablespoons basil, shredded

2 large aubergines
4 tablespoons olive oil
1½ lb/1 kg spinach, cleaned
2 cloves garlic, crushed
½ lb/250 g cottage cheese
3 tablespoons Parmesan cheese
1–2 tablespoons pesto

Method: Preheat oven to 190°C/375°F/gas mark 5.

Grill or roast the peppers until the skins are black and charred, cool, then peel, remove the seeds and slice into 4–6 pieces each.

Make the sauce: heat the oil and cook the onion for 5 minutes. Add the garlic and chilli and cook for 1 minute more, then pour in the tomatoes, add the sugar and season with salt and pepper to taste, and simmer for 30 minutes. Blend to a purée or rub through a sieve. Stir in the basil and check the seasoning.

Slice the aubergines lengthways into pieces about ¼ inch/½ cm thick. Season with salt and pepper. Heat a grill pan and brush with oil. Cook the aubergine slices until coloured on each side and soft. Brush with more oil if needed. Remove and cool.

Remove the stalks from the spinach. quickly stir-fry, drain and cool. Mix with the crushed garlic, cheeses and seasoning.

Lay 8 aubergine slices on a baking tray, cover evenly with the spinach mixture, add a layer of yellow and red peppers, spread with pesto and top with a slice of aubergine. Brush with olive oil and cover lightly with greaseproof paper or foil. Bake for 5–10 minutes to heat through.

To serve: serve with the sauce poured around. Garnish with basil leaves.
To accompany: a leafy green salad and herb or garlic bread.
Wine: Salice Salentino or another south Italian red.

Turkey medallions (serves 8)

1½ lb/700 g turkey breast
Purée
1 lb/450 g potatoes, peeled
12 oz/350 g celeriac, peeled
2 fl oz/55 ml milk
2 fl oz/55 ml cream
1 oz/25 g butter
salt, freshly ground black pepper

2 tablespoons olive oil
1 shallot, finely chopped
3 oz/75 g air-dried ham, chopped

4 oz/110 g shitake mushrooms, sliced
1 green apple, peeled, cored and diced
2 teaspoons sage, chopped
Sauce
6 tablespoons white wine
4 fl oz/110 ml chicken or turkey stock
2 teaspoons soy sauce
freshly ground black pepper
2 tablespoons Madeira (optional)

Method: Preheat oven to 190°C/375°F/gas mark 5.

Slice the turkey into 12 slices about ½ in/1 cm thick, then cut these in half to give 24 little medallions.

Boil the potatoes in salted water for 15 minutes until soft. Drain and dry, then mash to a purée. Chop the celeriac and boil in salted water for 10 minutes. Drain, then mash to a purée and combine with the potatoes. Beat in the milk, cream and butter and season well.

Heat 1 tablespoon of oil and cook the shallot, ham, mushrooms and apple until tender. Add the sage, season and reserve.

Season the medallions with salt and pepper on each side. Heat the remaining oil in a frying pan and cook the turkey for 2 minutes each side until golden. Transfer to a baking sheet, cover lightly with foil and cook in the oven for 5–10 minutes. Pour the wine into the pan and boil for 2 minutes, then add the stock and simmer for 5 minutes. Add the soy sauce and pepper, and Madeira if using.

To serve: place a spoonful of shallot mixture in the centre of each plate, arrange 3 medallions around, spoon a little sauce over, add a spoonful of purée and garnish with sage leaves.

To accompany: French beans tossed in olive oil.

Wine: red Burgundy or Rioja Reserva.

Roast cod (serves 8)

8 fillets of cod, skin scaled
2 tablespoons olive oil
1 small onion, peeled and
    finely chopped
1 carrot, peeled and chopped
2 cloves garlic, peeled
3 pieces star anise
8 oz/225 g green lentils
1 mixed bunch parsley, fennel
    and thyme

1 strip orange zest
5 fl oz/150 ml white wine
Sauce
3 fl oz/75 g white wine
½ teaspoon saffron strands
4 fl oz/110 ml fish stock
    (optional)
½ pint/275 ml cream
1 oz/25 g butter
salt, freshly ground black
    pepper

Method: Preheat oven to 190°C/375°F/gas mark 5.

Trim the cod, removing any remaining bones.

Cook the lentils: heat the olive oil and cook the onion, carrot, garlic and star anise for 3 minutes. Add the lentils and stir well. Add the herbs, orange zest and wine and boil up, cover generously with water, bring back to the boil and simmer for about 30 minutes until tender. Season with salt and pepper towards the end of cooking time.

Make the sauce: warm the wine, add the saffron and leave to infuse and release its colour. Boil to reduce by about half, then add the stock if using and boil to reduce again. Add the cream and simmer for 5 minutes, then whisk in the butter and season to taste. Keep warm.

Heat 1 tablespoon of oil in a heavy pan, and cook the cod skin side down until crisp. Transfer to a baking sheet skin side up and roast for 5–8 minutes.

To serve: spoon the lentils on to individual plates, top with the cod and pour the sauce around.

To accompany: a basket of fresh, crusty bread and some small tomatoes roasted in the oven with olive oil.

Wine: Chinon or New World Pinot Noir, slightly cool.

Char-grilled lamb steaks (serves 8)

8 lamb steaks, about ½ inch/
  1cm thick, cut from top of
  leg, boned

Marinade
4 tablespoons red wine
1 clove garlic, peeled and finely
  chopped
1 small onion, peeled and
  sliced
3 sprigs rosemary
3 slices root ginger
2 tablespoons soy sauce
½ teaspoon crushed black
  pepper

Plum chutney
½ lb/225 g red plums, stoned
  and quartered
½ inch/1cm piece root ginger,
  peeled and finely chopped
½ red chilli, seeded and finely
  chopped
1 red pepper, seeded and
  chopped
1 red onion, peeled and
  chopped
3 tablespoons sugar
3 fl oz/75 ml red wine
salt, freshly ground black
  pepper
1 tablespoon olive oil

Note: Steaks need to marinate for 4–24 hours.

Method: Trim the steaks leaving a small border of fat, and slash the fat to prevent curling up on the grill. Combine the ingredients for the marinade in a shallow dish, add the steaks and turn to coat well. Cover and leave for at least 4 hours.

Make the chutney: combine all the ingredients in a saucepan and simmer for 20–30 minutes. Taste and add more sugar if needed. Cool.

Cook the lamb: heat a barbecue or grillpan. Remove the lamb from the marinade, brush the grill with oil and cook the steaks for about 4 minutes each side, turning once, and brushing with the marinade.

To serve: serve with the chutney.

To accompany: baked potatoes, the inside scooped out, mixed with chopped chives, blue cheese and a little cream, re-filled and baked again until golden.

Wine: Barossa Shiraz or Cabernet-Shiraz blend.

Pheasant pie (serves 8)

8 oz/225 g pheasant meat
6 oz/175 g chicken
½ oz/10 g butter
2 shallots, peeled and finely
chopped
2 teaspoons thyme, finely
chopped
1 clove garlic, peeled and finely
chopped
2 oz/50 g wild mushrooms,
sliced

5 oz/150 g potato, peeled and
sliced very thinly
2 tablespoons truffle oil
salt, freshly ground black
pepper
6 oz/175 g puff pastry
flour to roll out
1 egg
5 fl oz/150 ml cream

Method: Preheat oven to 200°C/400°F/gas mark 6.

Remove any skin and bone from the pheasant and chicken and shred the meats finely with a sharp knife. Do not mince. Place in a large mixing bowl.

Heat the butter in a small pan and cook the shallots, thyme, garlic and wild mushrooms for about 4 minutes. Cool, then add to the meat. Add the potato slices and truffle oil to the meat mixture and mix thoroughly by hand, seasoning generously with salt and pepper.

Cut the pastry in half. Roll out 1 piece thinly and cut out an 8 inch/10 cm circle using a plate or lid as a guide. Roll out the other piece of pastry and cut a slightly larger circle. Brush this circle with beaten egg and mark carefully like the spokes of a wheel, using a small knife and being careful not to cut through the pastry.

Lay the smaller circle on a baking tray and brush the edge with egg. Spoon the filling into the centre in a dome shape without pressing down. Cover with the other, glazed pastry circle and seal the edges very well.

Bake for 20 minutes. Meanwhile, boil the cream to reduce to about one-third of its original volume. Remove the pie after 20 minutes and cut a small circle from the centre of the lid. Pour in the cream, replace the lid and return to the oven for 5 minutes. Cool slightly before serving.

To serve: cut into wedges like a cake.

To accompany: serve on its own or with some leeks cooked in red wine.

Wine: vintage rosé Champagne; or more conventionally, mature St Émilion.

Escalope of chicken with basil and lemon (serves 8)

6 chicken breasts, boned and skinned
salt, freshly ground black pepper
3 tablespoons olive oil

1 clove garlic, peeled and crushed
zest and juice 1 lemon
3 tablespoons basil, shredded
6 tablespoons chicken stock

Method: Cut the chicken breasts into thin slices through the thickness of the meat, making 3 small escalopes from each breast. Flatten slightly to an even thickness and season with salt and pepper.

Heat 1 tablespoon of olive oil in a large frying pan, cook the escalopes quickly, 2 or 3 at a time, for about 2 minutes on each side. Transfer to a warmed plate as they cook.

Add the garlic, lemon, basil and stock to the pan and boil vigorously to reduce well. Season to taste, then remove from the heat and stir in the remaining olive oil.

To serve: pour the sauce over the chicken and serve.

To accompany: sliced courgettes tossed with chives and butter and a touch of chilli.

Wine: Verdicchio, Pinot Grigio or Pinot Bianco.

Aromatic vegetable couscous (serves 8)

Couscous
12 oz/350 g couscous
salt
2 tablespoons olive oil
2 teaspoons cumin, ground
1 teaspoon paprika
1 teaspoon cinnamon, ground
2 oz/50 g raisins
2 oz/50 g sunflower seeds,
  toasted

Vegetable casserole
2 tablespoons olive oil
2 onions, peeled and finely
  chopped
2 aubergines, diced
2 courgettes, diced
2 small carrots, peeled and
  diced
1 red pepper, cored, seeded and
  diced
1 green pepper, cored, seeded,
  diced
1 yellow pepper, cored, seeded,
  diced
1 lb/450 g plum tomatoes,
  peeled and chopped
4 cloves garlic, peeled and
  finely chopped
salt, freshly ground black
  pepper
1–2 teaspoons sugar
zest and juice 1 lemon
3 tablespoons chopped fresh
  mint

Yoghurt sauce
6 fl oz/160 ml natural yoghurt
2 cloves garlic, peeled and
  crushed with ½ teaspoon salt

Chilli dressing
1 red chilli, seeded and finely
  chopped
2 cloves garlic, peeled and
  finely crushed
1 tablespoon tomato purée
1 tablespoon sugar
juice ½ lemon
6 tablespoons olive oil

Method: Prepare the couscous: place the grain in a bowl. Add
the salt, olive oil and spices and cover with boiling water. Stir in
the raisins and sunflower seeds and leave to stand for 5 minutes.
Mix lightly with a fork after about 2 minutes.

Make the casserole: heat the oil in a large casserole and cook the
onions for 5 minutes. Add the aubergine, courgettes and carrots and
cook for 10 minutes. Add the peppers, tomatoes and garlic, season
well, cover and cook for 10–15 minutes until the vegetables are
tender. Stir in the mint and lemon and check the seasoning.

Stir the garlic and salt into the yoghurt and chill. Combine all the ingredients for the dressing and mix well. It should look separated. Cover the couscous and heat in a medium oven (170–180°C/350–375°F/gas mark 4–5) for 10–15 minutes. Reheat the vegetable casserole if necessary.

To serve: make a base of couscous on each plate with a spoon or using a mould. Spoon on the vegetables and top with yoghurt. Sprinkle the chilli dressing around the plate. Garnish with herbs.

To accompany: warm pitta bread or French bread and a salad of young spinach.

Wine: Corbières, Fitou or Coteaux du Languedoc.

Stir-fry beef (serves 8)

2 lb/900 g beef fillet
2 heads broccoli
4 tablespoons vegetable oil
1 large onion, peeled and sliced
2 red peppers, seeds removed, sliced
2 yellow peppers, seeds removed, sliced

1 tablespoon root ginger, finely chopped
4 tablespoons dry sherry
6 fl oz/160 ml stock or water
2 tablespoons soy sauce
2 tablespoons tomato ketchup
1 red chilli, seeded
2 tablespoons sesame oil
3 tablespoons toasted sesame seeds

Method: Cut the fillet into ½ inch/3 mm pieces and slice across the grain into strips. Cut the broccoli into small florets, peel the stalk and slice thinly.

Heat 2 tablespoons vegetable oil in a large, deep frying-pan or wok. Fry the beef in 2 or 3 batches over a high heat, stirring and mixing all the time, until well coloured and tender, about 4 minutes each batch. Add the broccoli, onion and peppers with more oil if needed, and stir-fry for 3–4 minutes, until the onion just starts to colour. Return the beef to the pan with the ginger, sherry, stock, soy, ketchup and chilli. Bring gently to the boil and simmer to heat through. Add the sesame oil and sprinkle with seeds.

To accompany: Steamed rice scented with orange zest.

Wine: Australian Shiraz or Californian Zinfandel.

Venison medallions with brambles (serves 8)

2 lb/1 kg fillet of venison

Sauce

2 tablespoons olive oil
1 small onion, peeled and
  chopped
1 small carrot, peeled and
  chopped
1 stalk celery, chopped
2 cloves garlic, peeled
1 bunch parsley, thyme,
  rosemary, marjoram
½ pint/275 ml red wine
1 teaspoon black pepper,
  lightly crushed
1 pint stock or water

4 cloves
½ cinnamon stick
½ teaspoon allspice berries
12 oz/350 g blackberries
1 oz butter

Potato purée

1½ lb/700 g potatoes
salt
1 oz/25 g butter
3 fl oz/75 ml cream
4 tablespoons parsley, finely
  chopped
1 oz butter

Method: Cut the venison into 16 small medallions, trim to give a good shape, about ½ inch/1cm thick. Chop the trimmings and reserve.

Make the sauce: in a large, wide pan heat the oil and add the venison trimmings; cook until coloured then add the chopped vegetables and cook until well browned, about 10 minutes. Add the garlic and herbs, then pour in the wine and reduce by half. Add the pepper and stock or water and simmer for 30 minutes. Add the spices and half of the blackberries to the sauce and continue to cook for 20 minutes more. Pass through a sieve and boil rapidly until concentrated and dark in colour. Season and reserve. Just before serving, reheat the sauce, heat the butter and quickly sauté the remaining blackberries to heat through. Add to the sauce.

Make the potato purée: peel the potatoes and cook in boiling salted water until tender. Drain and dry over heat, then mash to a purée. Beat in the butter, cream, parsley and seasoning. Keep warm.

Heat a frying-pan. Season the medallions on both sides and cook for about 3 minutes each side. Leave to rest on a warm plate for 5 minutes.

To serve: serve 2 medallions per person garnished with a spoonful of parsley potato and sauce spooned over each piece of meat.

To accompany: lightly cooked, shredded cabbage flavoured with smoked bacon and crushed juniper berries.

Wine: Northern Rhône Côte Rôtie or mature Cornas.

Grilled chicken with vegetable noodles (serves 8)

8 chicken breasts, boned and skinned

Marinade

1 inch/2.5 cm piece root ginger, finely chopped

2 cloves garlic, peeled and finely chopped

2 teaspoons coriander, ground

zest and juice 1 lime

2 tablespoons honey

2 tablespoons soy sauce

freshly ground black pepper

2 tablespoons vegetable oil

Vegetable noodles

12 oz/350 g egg noodles

2 tablespoons vegetable oil

6 spring onions, peeled and sliced

2 cloves garlic, peeled and sliced

1 red chilli, seeded and chopped

½ cucumber, sliced into matchsticks

1 red pepper, seeded and sliced

6 oz/175 g mushrooms, preferably shitake, sliced

1 tablespoon soy sauce

1 tablespoon sesame oil

2 tablespoons fresh coriander, chopped

Note: The chicken needs to marinate for 2–8 hours.

Method: Make cuts in each chicken breast with a sharp knife, but do not cut right through the meat. Combine all the ingredients for the marinade . Add the chicken breasts, turning to coat evenly. Cover and leave for 2–8 hours. Cook the noodles as directed. Reserve.

In a large frying-pan, heat the vegetable oil and cook the spring onions, garlic and chilli for 2 minutes. Add the cucumber, pepper and mushrooms and cook for 8 minutes. Add the soy and sesame oil and remove from heat. Heat a grill pan or grill. Drain the chicken from its marinade, sieve the marinade into a small pan, add 6 tablespoons of water and boil rapidly to reduce to almost a glaze. Grill the chicken for 5 minutes each side. Leave to rest for 5 minutes on a warm plate. Reheat the vegetables, add the noodles and cook until very hot. Add the coriander.

To serve: arrange each chicken breast on top of a bed of noodles and vegetables and brush with the reduced marinade.

To accompany: a green salad.

Wine: Gewürztraminer from Alsace or the New World.

Oriental duck (serves 8)

1 duck, about 4–5 lb/2–2½ kg
salt, pepper
Spicing mixture
1 tablespoon 5-spice powder
1 tablespoon root ginger, finely chopped
2 cloves garlic, finely chopped
3 tablespoons soy sauce

4 tablespoons vegetable oil
3 cloves smoked garlic, peeled and sliced

1 inch/2.5 cm piece root ginger, sliced and shredded
1 green pepper, seeded and sliced
1 red pepper, seeded and sliced
2 leeks
1½ tablespoons salted black beans
2 tablespoons soy sauce
2 tablespoons sherry vinegar
1 tablespoon sugar
2 teaspoons chilli sauce

Note: The duck needs to be left in spices for 4 hours or overnight.

Method: Preheat oven to 190°C/375°F/gas mark 5.

Cut the duck in half through the back and breast bones and season well with salt and pepper. Heat a roasting pan and cook the duck halves, skin side down, until the fat starts to run. Transfer to the oven and cook for 45 minutes, turning once.

Cool the duck slightly, then combine all the ingredients for the spicing mixture and rub into the duck. Leave for 4 hours or overnight, refrigerating when cold.

Pull the duck meat off the bones and tear into fine shreds. Heat the oil in a wok or large frying-pan and fry the garlic, ginger, peppers and leeks for 2 minutes. Add the duck meat with all the remaining ingredients and stir-fry vigorously for 2–3 minutes. Serve at once.

To accompany: steamed rice and a side dish of stir-fried broccoli and mushrooms.

Wine: Fleurie.

Grilled red mullet with tomato and tapenade (serves 8)

Tapenade
20 black olives
2 cloves garlic, peeled
1 tablespoon capers
2 tablespoons parsley
6 anchovy fillets
juice 1 lemon
freshly ground black pepper
2–4 tablespoons olive oil
Sauce
1 pint/570 ml white wine
½ teaspoon saffron strands
10 tablespoons olive oil
Mullet
8 large fillets red mullet

1 red onion, peeled and sliced
4 cloves garlic, peeled
1 teaspoon fennel seeds
1 strip orange zest
2 pieces star anise
3 stalks fennel, reserving
    fronds for garnish
2–4 teaspoons tomato purée
Roasted tomatoes
1 lb/450 g plum tomatoes,
    peeled and cut in half
1 tablespoon olive oil
2 tablespoons balsamic vinegar
salt, freshly ground black
    pepper

Method: Preheat oven to 190°C/375°F/gas mark 5 for the tomatoes.

Make the tapenade: remove the stones from the olives. Chop the olives, garlic, capers, parsley and anchovies together until very fine. Add the lemon juice, seasoning and olive oil to get a rich paste. Store in a small jar until using—covered with olive oil it keeps well in the fridge.

Make the sauce: heat a little of the wine and soak the saffron strands to release colour. Gently heat 2 tablespoons of olive oil and cook the onion until soft but without letting it colour. Add the garlic, fennel seeds, orange zest, star anise, herbs, tomato purée, saffron mixture and the remaining wine. Bring to the boil and simmer for 40 minutes. Pass through a sieve and add the remaining olive oil. Check seasoning.

Roast the tomatoes: heat the olive oil in a small dish, add the tomatoes, season and transfer to the oven for 30 minutes. Add the balsamic vinegar and gently turn the tomatoes in the mixture to coat them.

Cook the mullet: cut the fillets in half and season with salt and pepper. Heat the olive oil in a non-stick pan and cook the fish for 2–3 minutes each side. Remove and leave to rest on a warm plate for 5 minutes.

To serve: gently warm the sauce without allowing it to boil. Reheat the tomatoes if necessary. Place a few tomato pieces on each plate, add 2 pieces of fish, top with a spoonful of tapenade and pour the sauce around. Decorate with sprigs of fennel.

To accompany: potato purée flavoured with garlic and olive oil and some grilled courgettes, served separately; or, more simply, some good bread.

Wine: New World Pinot Noir.

Roast lamb with beans (serves 8)

1 leg lamb, with hip and thigh
  bones removed
freshly ground black pepper
1 tablespoon olive oil
Beans
12 oz/350 g dried haricot
  beans, soaked overnight
3 tablespoons olive oil
1 onion, peeled and chopped
2 carrots, peeled and chopped

1 stick celery, chopped
1 head or bulb garlic, cut in
  half
1 bunch parsley, thyme,
  rosemary
6 fl oz/175 g white wine
3 tablespoons basil, shredded
salt
½ pint/275 ml lamb or
  chicken stock

Note: Haricot beans need to be soaked overnight

Method: Preheat oven to 190°C/375°F/gas mark 5.

Trim excess fat from the lamb, season with pepper and rub the inside with olive oil. Roll and tie into shape.

Drain the beans. Heat the olive oil in a large saucepan and cook the chopped vegetables for 3–5 minutes. Add the beans and mix well. Add the garlic, bunch of herbs and wine and bring to the boil. Cover with water, put on a lid and cook for 40–60 minutes until the beans are tender. Season towards the end of cooking time. Finally stir in the basil.

Meanwhile, cook the lamb: heat a roasting pan and brown the lamb, seasoning with salt and pepper. Roast for 40 minutes. Remove from the oven, wrap in foil and leave to rest for 20 minutes. Add the stock to the roasting pan and boil to reduce by half, seasoning to taste.

To serve: carve the lamb and serve with the beans and gravy.

To accompany: a dish of carrots cooked with butter and shallots

Wine: Fronsac or Canon-Fronsac.

Thai chicken curry (serves 8)

2 lb/1 kg chicken thighs,
  boned and skinned
2 tablespoons vegetable oil
2 onions, peeled and finely
  chopped
3 cloves garlic, peeled and
  sliced
2 green peppers, seeded and
  sliced
1 tablespoon tomato purée

1–2 tablespoons Thai red curry
  paste
¼ pint/150 ml chicken stock
½ pint/300 ml coconut cream
juice 1 lime
4 tablespoons fresh coriander,
  chopped
salt, freshly ground black
  pepper

Method: Cut the chicken into 1 inch/2.5 cm cubes.

Heat the oil in a frying pan and brown the chicken, turning regularly until browned on all sides. Remove the chicken and add the onions, garlic and peppers to the pan. Cook for 5–10 minutes until the onions are starting to colour. Return the chicken to the pan with the tomato purée and curry paste and stir-fry for about 5 minutes over a gentle heat.

Add the chicken stock and coconut cream and simmer for 15 minutes or until the chicken is tender. Remove the chicken and vegetables with a draining spoon to a serving dish.

Simmer the sauce to reduce to a light coating consistency, then add the lime juice, coriander and seasoning. Pour the sauce over the chicken and serve.

To accompany: steamed jasmine rice moulded into little turrets with ramekins or flan rings.

Wine: South Australian Chardonnay.

Sea bass with coriander and courgettes (serves 8)

Courgette flans

2 tablespoons olive oil

1 large onion, peeled and finely chopped

2 cloves garlic, peeled and finely chopped

2 lb/1 kg young courgettes, grated and dried

3 tablespoons chives, chopped

2 eggs, beaten

6 tablespoons cream

3 tablespoons Gruyère cheese, grated

salt, freshly ground black pepper

Sauce

4 fl oz/110 ml white wine

4 fl oz/110 ml fish stock

stalks from coriander

½ inch/1 cm piece root ginger, sliced

1 strip lemon peel

1 teaspoon black peppercorns

½ pint/275 ml cream

2 tablespoons fresh coriander, chopped

1 oz/25 g butter

2 tomatoes, peeled, seeded and chopped

8 fillets of sea bass, about 6 oz each, skin scaled

salt, freshly ground black pepper

1 tablespoon olive oil

Method: Preheat oven to 180°C/350°F/gas mark 4.

Prepare the courgette flans: heat the oil in a large frying pan. Add the onion and cook for 5 minutes, then stir in the garlic and courgette and cook, stirring frequently for 5–10 minutes. Transfer to a bowl and add the chives, eggs, cream, 2 tablespoons of cheese and season to taste. Brush 8 small tartlet tins or ramekins with oil and spoon in the courgette mixture. Sprinkle the top with the remaining cheese. Bake for 15–20 minutes.

Make the sauce: place the wine, stock, coriander stalks, ginger, lemon peel and peppercorns in a saucepan and reduce to about a third of its volume. Add the cream and simmer until lightly thickened, pass through a sieve and reheat. Season, add the coriander and whisk in the butter. Cover with the lid and take off the heat. Scatter in the chopped tomato just before serving.

Season the fish. Heat the olive oil in a large pan. Cook the fish skin side down for 5 minutes. Turn and cook 3–4 minutes more.

Leave to rest for 5 minutes.

To serve: unmould the courgette flans onto individual plates, add the fish and garnish with the sauce and coriander sprigs.

To accompany: steamed potatoes or crusty bread.

Wine: Mature white Burgundy.

Hake with potatoes and mustard (serves 8)

Spinach
2 lb/1 kg spinach, cleaned
1 tablespoon olive oil
Potatoes
1½ lb/700 g new potatoes
salt
2 shallots, peeled and finely
  chopped
2 tablespoons chives, chopped
2 tablespoons parsley, chopped
4 tablespoons white wine
1 tablespoon olive oil
Mustard dressing
juice 1 lemon

3 tablespoons white wine
2–3 tablespoons wholegrain
  mustard
1 teaspoon sugar
5 fl oz/150 ml olive oil

1½ lb/700 g fillet hake, skinned
1 tablespoon olive oil
½ oz/10 g butter
1 tablespoon chives, chopped
1 tablespoon flat parsley

salt, freshly ground black
  pepper

Method: Preheat oven to 190°C/375°F/gas mark 5.

Heat the oil in a wok or very large pan and stir-fry the spinach rapidly for about 3 minutes until just wilted. Season well. Reserve. Boil the potatoes until tender, cool slightly and then slice. Add the shallots, herbs, wine, olive oil and season. Do not break up the potato slices.

Make the dressing: gently heat the lemon juice, wine, mustard and sugar. Remove from heat and whisk in the oil. Season.

Cut the fish into 8 portions and season. Heat the oil and butter in a shallow flameproof dish, add the fish and colour on one side. Bake in the oven for 6–8 minutes. Reheat the spinach and potatoes.

To serve: Place spinach on each plate. Top with a fillet of fish. Place potato around the edge and spoon the dressing all over. Decorate with chives and parsley.

Wine: White Bordeaux.

Pasta layered with feta cheese (serves 8)

Tomato sauce

2 tablespoons olive oil
1 large onion, peeled and
    chopped
3 cloves garlic, peeled and
    chopped
2 cans plum tomatoes
2 sundried tomatoes
rind from a piece of Parmesan
    cheese (optional)
1 mixed bunch parsley, thyme,
    basil
salt, freshly ground black pepper

1 teaspoon sugar
3–4 tablespoons basil, shredded
salt
juice 1 lemon
12 oz/350 g penne rigate
2 tablespoons olive oil
2 red peppers, grilled, skinned,
    and seeded
1 lb/450 g feta cheese
black pepper
3 tablespoons Parmesan
    cheese, grated

Method: Preheat oven to 190°C/375°F/gas mark 5.

Make the tomato sauce: heat the oil and cook the onion and garlic for 5 minutes. Add the tomatoes, sundried tomatoes and Parmesan piece, then add the herbs and season to taste. Simmer for 30 minutes. Remove the Parmesan and blend to a purée. Check seasoning and add the basil.

Cook the penne: bring a large pan of water to the boil, add salt, lemon juice and penne and cook the pasta for 8–10 minutes or as directed. Drain, rinse with cold water and toss with olive oil.

Make the filling: cut the peppers into slices and crumble the cheese into large cubes.

Mix the penne with the tomato sauce, reserving a little of the sauce to finish the dish. Check the seasoning again then spoon half the pasta into an ovenproof dish about 2 inches/5 cm deep. Spoon over the cheese and peppers and season with black pepper. Cover with the remaining pasta. Spread the remaining sauce over the top and sprinkle with the cheese. Bake for 20 minutes.

To accompany: a green salad.

Wine: well-made red Valdepeñas or unoaky Cencibel from southern Spain.

Pasta with salmon and green vegetables (serves 8)

1 lb/450 g salmon fillet, skinned

2 tablespoons olive oil

1 oz/25 g butter

6 spring onions, sliced

4 oz/110 g fresh or frozen peas

2 small courgettes, sliced

4 oz/110 g mange-tout, trimmed

salt, freshly ground black pepper

4 tablespoons white wine

8 oz/225 g ricotta cheese

3 tablespoons basil, shredded

2 tablespoons chives, finely chopped

juice 1 lemon

1 lb/450 g tagliatelle, fresh or dried

4 tablespoons olive oil

Method: Cut the salmon into pieces. Heat the oil and butter and cook the spring onions, peas, and courgettes for 5 minutes. Add the mange-tout and cook for 2–3 minutes. Season and add the wine. Add the salmon and simmer for 1–2 minutes.

Break up the ricotta and add to the fish and vegetables with the herbs. Heat gently for 1–2 minutes, then recheck the seasoning.

Meanwhile, bring a large pan of water to the boil, add salt and lemon juice and cook the pasta for 3–4 minutes for fresh or as directed for dry. Drain and toss with the olive oil and seasoning. Reheat the fish mixture if necessary and mix carefully with the pasta.

To accompany: crusty bread

Wine: Pinot Blanc.

Jambalaya (serves 8)

4 tablespoons olive oil
½ chicken, cut in 6 pieces
12 oz/350 g large prawns, boiled
½ lb/225 g chorizo sausage, chopped
4 oz/110 g bacon, chopped
4 oz/100g smoked ham, cubed
2 tablespoons olive oil
1 onion, peeled and chopped
4 cloves garlic, peeled and chopped

2 sticks celery, chopped
1 green pepper, seeded and chopped
12 oz/350 g long-grain rice
½ teaspoon cloves, ground
6 tablespoons white wine
1 can plum tomatoes
2 tablespoons tomato purée
3 sprigs thyme
1½ pints/900 ml chicken stock
12 black olives, stoned

Method: Heat the oil and brown the chicken to colour well on all sides. Remove from the pan into a large bowl. Add the prawns and cook quickly until slightly golden. Remove to the bowl, then add the chorizo and colour. Remove to the bowl with the chicken and prawns.

Cook the bacon and ham in the remaining oil for 1–2 minutes. Add the onion, garlic, celery and pepper and stir-fry for about 4 minutes. Add the rice and stir in. Add the cloves, 1 pint/500 ml wine, tomatoes, tomato purée and thyme and 1 pint stock, return the chicken to the pan and bring to the boil. Season, cover and simmer for 20 minutes, adding more stock if needed. Add the olives and cook uncovered for 5–10 minutes more.

To serve: transfer to a shallow serving dish.

To accompany: s colourful mixed bean salad and some bread.

Wine: Reserve Sauvignon Blanc from Chile, or fruity, Garnacha-based Navarra red.

Bean casserole (serves 8)

12 oz/350 g mixed beans—red kidney beans, black eye, haricot, soaked overnight
2 tablespoons olive oil
2 large onions, peeled andchopped
2 carrots, peeled and chopped
3 sticks celery, sliced
2 peppers, seeded and sliced
3 cloves garlic, peeled and chopped
1 red chilli, seeded and finely chopped
2 teaspoons paprika
2 tablespoons tomato purée

1 can tomatoes
4 fl oz white wine
2 teaspoons sugar
salt, freshly ground black pepper
2 tablespoons chopped parsley
2 tablespoons chopped oregano
Topping
1 French stick
1–2 tablespoons wholegrain mustard
2 oz/50 g butter
4 tablespoons sesame seeds

Note: The beans need to soak overnight.

Method: Preheat oven to 180°C/350°F/gas mark 4.

Cook the beans in plenty of water, boiling rapidly for 10 minutes, then steadily, covered, for 1 hour.

Heat the oil and cook the onions, carrots, celery and peppers until just beginning to turn golden. Add the garlic and chilli and cook for 1–2. Drain the cooked beans and add to the onion mixture with the paprika, tomato purée, tomatoes, sugar and wine. Season and add about ¼ pint/150 ml water and the herbs. Cover and bake for 1 hour. Check occasionally that the casserole is not drying out, adding more water if needed.

Cut the bread into slices. Mix the mustard and butter and spread over the bread. Arrange the slices over the top of the casserole, sprinkle with the sesame seeds and bake uncovered for 15 minutes until golden.

To serve: straight from the casserole.

To accompany: a simple green salad.

Wine: Periquita-based Portuguese red.

Braised beef (serves 8)

3 lb/1.25 kg thick flank beef
salt, freshly ground black
  pepper
3 tablespoons olive oil
2 onions, peeled and chopped
4 cloves garlic

4 oz/100 g Parma ham,
  chopped
3 sprigs rosemary
1 can plum tomatoes
2 tablespoons tomato purée
1 pint/570 ml red wine

Method: Preheat oven to 140°C/275°F/gas mark 1.

Cut the beef into 2–3 oz/50–75 g pieces, trimming away excess fat. Season with salt and pepper.

Heat the olive oil in a frying-pan. Brown the meat thoroughly on all sides, cooking in batches to get a good colour. Transfer to a casserole. Add the onions, garlic and ham to the pan and cook until well coloured, about 8 minutes. Add about 4 tablespoons of water, boil and stir and scrape the contents of the pan into the casserole with the meat. Add the rosemary, tomatoes, purée and wine. Bring to the boil, season and cover. Reduce heat to simmer and transfer to the oven for 2–2½ hours. Check the meat from time to time, turning the pieces in the juice.

Remove the meat to a serving dish and if necessary boil the juices to concentrate. Check the seasoning and spoon the juices over the meat.

To serve: serve straight from the casserole.

To accompany: French beans and braised celery.

Wine: Barolo or Barbaresco, 6–10 years old, depending on maker and year.

A sweet wine is often an excuse for a traditional or 'nursery' pudding.

Pear and walnut tarts (serves 8)

Pastry
7 oz/200 g plain flour, sifted
1 teaspoon cinnamon, ground
4 oz/110 g butter, diced
4 oz/110 g castor sugar
1 egg
2 oz/50 g walnuts, finely
   chopped

4 large ripe pears
juice ½ lemon
4–6 tablespoons sugar
2–3 tablespoons ground
   almonds
1 egg white
3 tablespoons castor sugar

Method: Preheat oven to 200°C/400°F/gas mark 6.

Make the pastry: mix the flour and cinnamon and spread on the work top. Make a well in the centre, add the butter, sugar and egg and work together with a palette knife, gradually drawing in the flour. Add the walnuts just before the mixture forms a dough. Knead lightly then wrap in greaseproof paper and chill for 1 hour.

Peel, core and halve the pears. Sprinkle with lemon juice and sugar. Roll out about two-thirds of the pastry and line 8 tartlet tins. Sprinkle the base of each with ground almonds and place a pear half in each. Lightly mix up the egg white and brush a little around the edge of each pastry. Roll out the remaining pastry and cut 8 circles to cover each tart. Seal the edges well and make 1 or 2 incisions in the top of each with the point of a knife. Brush with the remaining egg white and sprinkle with sugar. Bake for 20–25 minutes.

Wine: Jurançon moelleux.

Chocolate truffle (serves 8)

Sponge
2 eggs
2 oz/50 g castor sugar
10 oz/275 g flour
½ oz/10 g cocoa
½ oz/10 g ground almonds

Syrup
5 oz/150 g sugar
5 fl oz/150 ml water
2–3 tablespoons brandy
Chocolate cream
12 oz/350 g good quality dark chocolate
12 fl oz/335 ml cream
cocoa powder for dusting

Method: Preheat oven to 180°C/350°F/gas mark 4.

Make the sponge: whisk the eggs and sugar to a thick, mousse-like consistency. Sieve the flour and cocoa and mix with the ground almonds, then fold into the eggs. Place a sheet of non-stick baking paper on an oven tray and spread the sponge mixture on this in a thin, even layer. Bake for 12–15 minutes. Cool.

Make the syrup: bring the sugar and water to the boil to dissolve the sugar, then cool. Stir in the brandy.

Take a 10 inch/25 cm cake ring or spring-form tin. Trim the sponge to *exactly* the size of the bottom of the tin or ring and place inside. Brush thoroughly with syrup.

Carefully melt the chocolate in a bowl over hot water. Whisk the cream until just holding a shape but still very soft. Fold together the chocolate and cream, working quickly but lightly. Pour the mixture into the tin on top of the sponge and level the top by gently shaking and tapping the tin. Chill until set.

Take a tea towel and rinse in very hot water, then apply it to the sides of the tin to loosen the cream. Remove the tin. Dust the top with cocoa.

To serve: serve in thin slices. When cutting the truffle, dip the knife in hot water between each slice to give a neat cut.

Wine: Banyuls.

Gooseberry flan (serves 8)

8 oz/225 g sweet pastry (see page 153)

flour

Filling

10 fl oz/280 ml cream

1 vanilla pod

2 eggs

5 oz/150 g castor sugar

1½ oz/40 g flour

1 lb/450 g gooseberries, washed, dried, topped and tailed

icing sugar for dusting

Method: Preheat oven to 200°C/400°F/gas mark 6.

Roll out the pastry and line a 9 inch/23 cm metal flan tin. Trim the edges neatly and prick the base with a fork. Chill for at least 30 minutes, then bake the pastry blind for 5–8 minutes until the edges are lightly coloured and the base is dry. Cool.

Make the filling: heat the cream and vanilla. Whisk the eggs with the sugar and flour then pour the hot cream mixture onto the egg mixture, whisking well. Cool, then remove the vanilla.

Place the gooseberries in the pastry case. Pour over the custard, lower the oven to 190°C/375°F/gas mark 5, and bake for 20–30 minutes.

To serve: serve warm or cold dusted with icing sugar.

Wine: Muscat de Frontignan.

Old-fashioned bakewell tart (serves 8)

8 oz/225 g sweet pastry (see
   page 153)
flour to roll out
Lemon crème anglaise
grated zest 1 lemon, blanched
12 fl oz/330 ml milk
4 egg yolks
4 oz/110 g castor sugar

Filling
4 oz/110 g butter
4 oz/110 g castor sugar
2 eggs
3 oz/75 g ground almonds
2 oz/50 g plain cake crumbs
zest 1 lemon
6 tablespoons raspberry jam

Method: Preheat oven to 200°C/400°F/gas mark 6.

Make the crème anglaise: place the blanched lemon zest and milk in a saucepan and bring to the boil. Whisk the yolks and sugar until thick and creamy, pour on the hot milk, return to a low heat—or place over hot water—and cook until just thickened. The mixture should just coat the back of a wooden spoon. Pass through a sieve and cool quickly, then chill.

Roll out the pastry and line a 9 inch/23 cm metal flan tin. Trim the edges neatly and prick the base with a fork. Chill for at least 30 minutes. Bake the pastry blind for 5–8 minutes. Cool.

Make the filling: cream the butter and sugar very thoroughly, then beat in the eggs, followed by the ground almonds and cake crumbs and the lemon zest.

Spread the base of the pastry with jam, then pipe over the filling or spread it carefully with a spatula. Lower the oven to 190°C/275°F/gas mark 5, and bake for 25 minutes. Cool slightly.

To serve: dust with icing sugar and serve with the crème anglaise.

Wine: Australian Botrytis Semillon.

Chocolate date and nut cake (serves 8)

2 tablespoons flour, sifted
1 teaspoon baking powder
1 teaspoon cinnamon
6 oz/175 g sugar
2 eggs
4 oz/110 g walnuts, chopped
8 oz/225 g dates, chopped

2 oz/50 g dark chocolate, grated

To decorate
6 fl oz/160 ml cream
2 tablespoons icing sugar
good quality dark, bitter chocolate in a block

Method: Preheat oven to 150°C/300°F/gas mark 2.

Mix flour, baking powder, ½ teaspoon cinnamon and 5 oz/150 g sugar. Whisk the eggs until fluffy and fold in the dry ingredients followed by the nuts, dates and chocolate. Line a 9 inch/23 cm tin with non-stick paper and pour in the cake mixture. Mix the remaining sugar and cinnamon and sprinkle over cake. Bake for 1 hour. Cool, then unmould.

Whisk the cream and sugar for the decoration and spread over the cake. Shave some large curls from the block of chocolate and scatter over the top.

Wine: Rutherglen Liqueur Muscat.

Melon slices with strawberry chantilly (serves 8)

Strawberry chantilly
8 oz/225 g strawberries, hulled and sliced
zest and juice 1 orange

8 fl oz/225 ml cream
1 egg white
1–2 oz/25–50 g castor sugar
1 ripe Galia melon

Method: Make the strawberry chantilly: sprinkle the strawberries with orange zest and juice. Whisk the cream. Whisk the egg white and fold into the cream with the sugar, tasting for sweetness. Fold in the strawberries and orange. Chill. Peel and slice the melon

To serve: serve the fanned melon slices with a mound of chantilly.

Wine: Asti Spumante or Moscato d'Asti.

Greengage fool (serves 8)

1 lb/450 g ripe greengages
2–3 oz/50–75 g castor sugar
2 oz/50 g butter

15 fl oz/425 ml cream
2 tablespoons Armagnac

Method: Halve and stone the greengages and combine with the sugar in a saucepan.

Heat gently until the juice runs from the fruit then cook until soft—about 10 minutes. Rub through a sieve and cool slightly. While the mixture is still warm whisk in the butter. Cool completely but do not chill. Whisk the cream and fold into the purée with the Armagnac.

Spoon the fool into individual glasses and chill until serving.

Wine: Muscat de Setúbal.

Poached pears with almond tuiles (serves 8)

Tuiles
6 oz/175 g flaked almonds
4 oz/110 g castor sugar
1 oz/25 g flour
4 egg whites
icing sugar for dusting
Pears
½ pint/275 ml white wine

6 oz sugar
1 vanilla pod
8 pears
Caramel sauce
4 oz/110 g sugar
4 tablespoons water
1 pint/570 ml cream

Note: Tuile mixture needs to be left for 2–3 hours.

Method: Make the tuiles: mix the almonds, sugar and flour with the egg whites. Leave for 2–3 hours. Preheat oven to 180°C/350°F/gas mark 4. Line some baking sheets with non-stick paper. Take tablespoons of the tuile mixture and spread out into very thin 3–4 inch/7–10 cm discs, spaced well apart, 3–4 on each tray. Bake for 5–6 minutes until golden. Remove from the baking tray at once and shape over a rolling pin, or similar broad curve, working quickly before the biscuits cool. Before serving, dust with icing sugar.

Cook the pears: place the wine, sugar and vanilla in a saucepan. Peel the pears, removing the core but leaving the stalk in place, and add to the pan. Add water to cover the pears, bring to the boil and simmer for 10–30 minutes depending on the ripeness of the pears. Cool, then chill.

Make the sauce: put the sugar and water in a heavy pan, heat to melt the sugar then boil rapidly to a rich caramel colour, pour in the cream and cook, stirring, until rich and smooth. Pour into a bowl and cool. Chill.

To serve: serve the pears with the sauce and tuiles.

Wine: Sauternes.

Plum crumble with cinnamon cream (serves 8)

Crumble mixture
6 oz/175 g flour
2 oz/50 g sliced almonds
4 oz/110 g brown sugar
4 oz/110 g butter
Plums
1 oz/25 g butter
2 lb/900 g ripe plums, halved
   and stoned

½ cinnamon stick
2 oz/50 g sugar
Cinnamon cream
3 fl oz/75 ml cream, whipped
5 fl oz/150 ml Greek yoghurt
1 teaspoon cinnamon
1 tablespoon dark honey

Method: Preheat oven to 190°C/375°F/gas mark 5.

Make the crumble mixture: mix the flour, nuts and sugar and lightly rub in the butter.

Cook the plums: heat the butter, add the plums, cinnamon and sugar and cook until almost tender. Remove the cinnamon and spoon into individual gratin dishes or tartlet tins. Sprinkle the crumble mixture on top of the plums and bake for 15 minutes.

Make the cinnamon cream: mix together the cream and yoghurt and fold in the cinnamon and honey. Chill.

To serve: serve in the gratin dishes, or unmoulded from the tartlet tins, with the cinnamon cream.

Wine: Tokay Aszú.

Warm walnut pudding with caramel (serves 8)

Pudding
flour and butter to line dishes
3½ oz/90 g butter
3 oz/75 g castor sugar
2 oz/50 g walnuts, finely
   chopped
2 eggs, separated
4 tablespoons breadcrumbs

2 tablespoons flour
Sauce
2 oz/50 g butter
4 oz/110 g soft brown sugar
5 fl oz/150 ml cream

Method: Preheat oven to 180°C/350°F/gas mark 4.

Make the pudding: butter and flour 8 small ramekins or soufflé dishes. Beat the butter until very light then whisk in the sugar. Add the walnuts and egg yolks and mix well. Fold in the breadcrumbs and flour. Whisk the egg whites and fold in, then spoon the mixture into the dishes and bake for 20 minutes.

Make the sauce: combine the butter, sugar and cream in a saucepan and heat until melted. Boil for 2–3 minutes. Cool but serve warm.

Remove the puddings from the oven and leave to stand for 5 minutes.

To serve: carefully unmould and serve with the sauce.

Wine: Mature Sauternes.

Caramel rice cream with dried fruit

Rice cream
4 oz/110 g short grain rice
1 pint/570 ml milk
1 vanilla pod, split
2 oz/50 g sugar
5 fl oz/150 ml cream
4 oz/110 g sugar for caramel

Dried fruit compote
8 oz/225 g dried apricots
6fl oz/160 ml Muscat wine
strip orange zest
4 cardamom pods
2 tablespoons honey

Note: The apricots need to be soaked overnight in wine. The rice cream needs to chill for 3–4 hours or overnight.

Method: Soak the apricots overnight in the wine. Next day, place them in a pan with the wine, orange zest, cardamom, honey and enough water to just cover. Simmer uncovered for 15 minutes until soft. Cool, then chill until ready to use.

Make the rice cream: place the rice, milk, vanilla and sugar in a saucepan and simmer very gently until cooked and creamy, about 45 minutes. Stir occasionally and check that it is not drying too much. Cool and remove the vanilla pod. Whisk the cream softly and fold into the cold rice. Spoon into small flan rings or little moulds. Chill for 3–4 hours or overnight.

Carefully unmould the rice creams and sprinkle the tops with an even coating of sugar. Glaze the sugar to a good caramel using a blow lamp or by placing the creams under a hot grill.

To serve: transfer to individual plates and garnish with some apricots in syrup.

Wine: Jurançon moelleux.

Crème brûlée with ginger (serves 8)

Crème
1 pint/570 ml cream
1 vanilla pod, split
8 egg yolks
4 oz/110 g castor sugar

Ginger filling
6–8 pieces stem ginger in
  syrup, chopped
Caramel topping
6 oz/175 g sugar

Note: The creams need to chill overnight.

Method: Make the crème: Put the cream and vanilla in a saucepan and bring to the boil, then remove from heat.

Whisk the egg yolks and sugar until creamy and light, then add to the cream, stirring all the time. Return to a very low direct heat or place over hot water and cook until rich and thick and coating the back of a spoon. Cool, then remove the vanilla.

Place a spoonful of chopped ginger, with its syrup, in each of 8 small ramekin or gratin dishes. Spoon in the cream and leave to cool completely, then chill overnight until set.

Sprinkle the creams with an even layer of sugar and glaze to a caramel either with a blow lamp or under the grill.

Wine: Californian late-harvested Riesling.

Tarte tatin (serves 8)

2 oz/50 g butter
5 oz/150 g castor sugar
4–6 dessert apples, peeled,
  cored and quartered
juice ½ lemon

6 oz/175 g puff pastry
flour to roll out
1 egg white
2 tablespoons castor sugar

Method: Preheat oven to 200°C/400°F/gas mark 6.

Select a heavy ovenproof frying-pan or shallow dish. Warm the butter and sugar in the pan. Place the apples in the pan, rounded side down. Sprinkle with lemon juice and cook over a moderate to high heat until the apples start to caramelise. Remove from heat.

Roll out the pastry and cut a circle the same size as the pan or dish. Cover the apples with the pastry, tucking the edges around the apples. Brush with egg white and sprinkle with sugar.

Bake for 30–40 minutes. Cool for 5 minutes. Then carefully invert the tart on to a plate. Cool slightly before serving.

Wine: Auslese Riesling.

Orange and almond cake (serves 8)

4 oz/110 g butter
4 oz/110 g castor sugar
zest and juice 1 orange
2 large eggs
4 oz/110 g ground almonds
2 oz/50 g flour, sifted

Syrup
6 oz/175 g sugar
zest 1 orange
juice 2 oranges
2 tablespoons orange liqueur
Caramelised orange zest
zest 1 orange, finely sliced
2 oz/50 g sugar

Method: Preheat oven to 180°C/350°F/gas mark 4.

Beat the butter and sugar until light and fluffy. Gradually beat in the eggs then fold in the almonds and flour. Line an 8 inch/20 cm tin with non-stick paper and spoon in the cake mixture. Bake for 25 minutes. Cool slightly in the tin, then turn out.

Combine the sugar and 2 fl oz/55 ml water with the orange zest and bring to the boil. Simmer for 1 minute then add the orange juice and liqueur, bring back to the boil and cool.

Caramelise the zest strips: blanch the zest in boiling water then place the zest in a saucepan, add the sugar and 3 fl oz/75 ml water and boil. Boil for about 8 minutes until the liquid has evaporated and the zest is shining and caramelised. Spread on a tray and cool.

While the cake is hot, stand in a shallow dish and pour over the syrup. Leave to cool and absorb the syrup spooning more syrup off the dish over the cake. Decorate with the zest.

To serve: serve cold.

Wine: Muscat de Samos.

Baked peaches with mascarpone and almonds (serves 8)

8 large, ripe peaches
Filling
4 oz/110 g mascarpone cheese
2 oz/50 g amaretti biscuits, broken
2 tablespoons candied orange peel, chopped

½ teaspoon mixed spice
1 egg white
1 oz/25 g castor sugar
½ oz/10 g butter to grease dish
6–8 tablespoons sweet wine or Marsala

Method: Preheat oven to 170°C/340°F/gas mark 3½.

Blanch and skin the peaches. Cut in half and remove the stones.

Make the filling: put the cheese into a bowl, add the amaretti, orange peel and mixed spice. Whisk the egg white until stiff, then whisk in the sugar until glossy and stiff and fold into the cheese mixture.

Arrange the peach halves in a buttered, shallow dish and fill the centres with the cheese mixture. Pour in the wine. Bake for 20–25 minutes, until the peaches are soft and the filling is set.

Wine: Marsala or Vin Santo.

Strawberry tarts (serves 8)

Sweet pastry
9 oz/250 g plain flour
4 oz/110 g butter, diced
4 oz/110 g icing sugar
1 egg
1 yolk
flour

Filling
8 oz/225 g fromage blanc,
    drained for at least 2 hours
    in a muslin-lined sieve
1–2 oz/25–50 g castor sugar
12 oz/350 g ripe strawberries
icing sugar for dusting

Note: The pastry needs to chill for 2 hours.

Method: Preheat oven to 200°C/400°F/gas mark 6.

Make the pastry: place the flour on the worktop and spread into a ring. Put the butter, sugar, eggs and egg yolk in the centre and work these together with a palette knife. Gradually work in the flour, chopping and crumbling the mixture, then press the whole lot into a dough, knead once or twice, wrap in clingfilm and refrigerate for 2 hours. (The pastry keeps for 1–2 weeks in the fridge and can be frozen.)

Alternatively, place the butter, sugar, eggs and egg yolk in a food processor or mixer, blend together, then gradually work in the flour, being careful not to overwork and removing the pastry from the machine before it forms a dough.

Flour a worktop and roll out the pastry. Line 8 x 2½–3 inch/6–7 cm tartlet tins, pricking the pastry well. Chill for at least 30 minutes. Bake the tartlets blind for 5–8 minutes. Cool.

Make the filling: when the cheese has drained, add the sugar and mix well. Remove the stalks from the strawberries and slice.

Shortly before serving spoon some filling into each tartlet, cover with strawberries and dust lightly with icing sugar.

Wine: Coteaux du Layon, preferably Bonnezeaux or Quarts-de-Chaume.

Mango sabayon (serves 8)

3–4 ripe mangoes
Sabayon
5 fl oz/150 ml muscat wine
grated zest and juice 1 lime

6 egg yolks
3 oz/75 g castor sugar
icing sugar for dusting

Method: Peel the mangoes and slice thinly. Arrange on a heatproof platter or individual dishes.

Make the sabayon: place the wine, lime zest and juice, egg yolks and sugar in a large bowl and whisk over hot water until the mixture gains about 3 times its volume and holds the trail of the whisk. Remove from heat and continue to whisk for 1–2 minutes.

Pour the sabayon over the mango slices and dust with icing sugar. Place the dish or dishes under the grill for 30 seconds, watching all the time, until the sugar glazes. Alternatively use a blow lamp, which is easier for individual plates.

Wine: Coteaux du Layon.

Bread and butter pudding (serves 8)

2 oz/50 g sultanas
4 tablespoons brandy
Custard mixture
½ pint/275 ml milk
5fl oz/150 ml cream
2 vanilla pods, split
strip orange zest

3 eggs
4 oz/110 g castor sugar
Bread
8 slices good quality yeast
  bread
2–3 oz/50–75 g butter

Method: Preheat oven to 180°C/350°F/gas mark 4.

Soak the sultanas in the brandy. Put the milk, cream, vanilla and orange into a saucepan and bring to the boil. Whisk the eggs and sugar, pour on the milk/cream mixture, mix well and leave to cool.

Cut the crusts from the bread, butter generously, then cut each slice into 4 triangles. Drain the sultanas, letting the brandy drain into the custard. Layer the bread into an oven dish, scattering the sultanas between the layers. Strain the custard through a sieve over the bread. Sprinkle with sugar. Stand in a roasting tin filled with 1 inch/2 cm of water and bake for 30 minutes.

Wine: Monbazillac.

Bananas baked with vanilla and apricot with coconut biscuits (serves 8)

Biscuits	*Bananas*
4 oz/110 g castor sugar	8 bananas
3 oz/75 g dessiccated coconut	zest and juice 1 orange
1 oz/25 g flour	1 oz/25 g butter
2 egg whites	2 oz/50 g castor sugar
butter	2 fl oz/55 ml apricot juice
icing sugar	1 vanilla pod

Note: The biscuit mixture needs to rest for 2 hours.

Method: Make the biscuit mixture: mix the sugar, coconut, flour and egg whites. Cover and leave to rest for 2 hours.

Preheat oven to 170°C/340°F/gas mark 3½. Line some baking trays with non-stick paper using the butter. Place teaspoonfuls of the biscuit mixture on the baking sheets spaced well apart. Spread out into very thin discs. Bake for 5–6 minutes until golden, cool slightly then remove to a rack to cool. Dust with icing sugar.

Peel the bananas and soak in the orange juice and zest. Butter a shallow gratin dish and sprinkle with sugar and apricot juice or purée. Split the vanilla pod and scoop out the seeds. Add the seeds and pod to the banana and juice mixture. Put the mixture in the dish and bake at 180°C/350°F/gas mark 4 for 7–10 minutes.

To serve: serve hot or warm with the fruit juices and biscuits.

Wine: Australian late-harvested Muscat.

Lemon syllabub with hazelnut shortbread (serves 8)

Hazelnut shortbread
4 oz/110 g flour
2 oz/50 g hazelnuts, roasted, skinned and chopped
4 oz/110 g butter, softened
2 oz/50 g castor sugar
icing sugar

Syllabub
1 pint/570 ml cream
4 tablespoons castor sugar
4 fl oz/110 ml white wine
zest and juice 2 lemons
3 egg whites
mint leaves

Method: Preheat oven to 170°C/340°F/gas mark 3½.

Make the shortbread dough: mix the flour and nuts, mix in the butter and castor sugar and work quickly to a light dough. Chill. The mixtutre keeps for 1 week in fridge.

Bake the biscuits: roll out the shortbread and line a shallow rectangular tray, 6 x 8 inches/15 x 20 cm. Mark the dough into biscuits and bake for 20 minutes until light golden. Cut through the markings while still warm, then leave to cool before removing from the tin. Dust with icing sugar.

Make the syllabub: whisk the cream until soft peaks form. Add the sugar then beat in the wine, lemon zest and juice. Taste and add a little more sugar if needed.

Whisk the egg whites and fold in. If about to serve, spoon into individual glasses, otherwise spoon into a large bowl, cover and refrigerate until ready to serve. Whisk lightly to restore texture just before spooning into serving glasses.

To serve: Decorate with mint leaves and serve with the short-bread biscuits.

Wine: Australian late-harvested Riesling.

INDEXES

[157]

Index to Recipes

Index of Wines with Recipes